W9-CQX-648

New Life in Dark Seas: Brick Books 25

New Life in Dark Seas:
Brick Books 25

edited by Stan Dragland

Brick Books

CANADIAN CATALOGUING IN PUBLICATION DATA

Main entry unter title:

New life in dark seas: Brick Books 25

ISBN 1-894078-10-1

1. Canadian poetry (English) – 20th century.*
I. Dragland, Stan, 1942–

PS8293.N483 2000   C811'.5408   C00-931450-4
PR9195.25.N483 2000

Copyright © the authors, 2000.

We acknowledge the support of the Canada Council for the Arts
for our publishing programme. The support of the Ontario Arts
Council is also gratefully acknowledged.

Cover image is after a photograph by Stan Dragland
of the type set for Peggy Dragišić's Fom the Medley.
Design is courtesy of Alan Siu, Sunville Printco Inc.

Typeset in Minion. The stock is acid-free Zephyr Antique laid.
Printed and bound by The Porcupine's Quill Inc.

Brick Books
431 Boler Road, Box 20081
London, Ontario N6K 4G6

brick.books@sympatico.ca

Contents

For the Reader

I wouldn't read this introduction if I were you. I'd leave right after this paragraph and open the book anywhere else. Go for the poems. That's what we're celebrating here – twenty-five years of Brick Books helping poetry see the light and find its readers. See the light; find the poems. You are very welcome here, by the way. Many thanks for joining us.

*

Everyone at Brick Books has strong feelings about poetry. We gather that about each other in conversation and by reading each others' writing about poetry. Some of us are poets ourselves, and the rest are eager readers of those poets. For a spell we were all resident in London, Ontario and met weekly, mostly to divvy up the jobs. Sometimes we didn't see eye to eye at those meetings, but differences never explicitly had to do with principles for accepting books and editing them. There is no Brick Books aesthetic articulated from inside. Maybe next anniversary we'll ask each of the editors what they think they're doing and see if there's any consensus.

Maybe not. None of us is travelling blind, but I think we would all resist defining poetry, which is really what declaring an aesthetic involves. Anyone who claims to know poetry well enough to hang out a publisher's shingle should be able to articulate the recognition factors, but we expect to stay this side of declaration. We hope to stay open. I hear in what I'm saying an echo of 'I don't know anything about art but I know what I like.' There's something to be said for that amateur perspective, in fact, though it's a shame when smart people get stuck in it.

I speak here as for the group of editors, but I'm leery of generalization about us and our taste. I would advise caution. I'd suggest thinking of perhaps untypical Brick books (David Bromige's *Tiny Courts in a world without scales*, Colin Browne's *Abraham*, Anne Carson's *Short Talks*, Michael Kenyon's *Rack of Lamb*, P.K. Page's *Hologram*) not as marginal but as central. Michael Ondaatje's *Elimination Dance/La danse éliminatoire* would crack any taxonomy by itself.

What we editors *have* learned, through practice, is how with some success to enter the creative process at an advanced stage – how to engage with intellect and intuition under the assumption that *nothing* in a manuscript of poems escapes scrutiny. Here's the sort of question that comes up when the poet herself has not asked it: should the punctuation in *this* text be consistent throughout (not necessarily obedient to handbook rules) or should it float and vary with local circumstances in particular poems – if indeed conventional punctuation marks are to be used at all (line breaks, vertical and horizontal spaces – there are other ways of notating syntax or rhythm). Everything depends on everything else in a manuscript, so the questions rise individually out of each book-to-be. It's why no editing system (even for a particular poetry editor) will kick in automatically, mechanically. At the same time, few of the questions are arcane because words and sentences and all the other materials of poetry are common to other sorts of discourse. The trick, if there is one, is in responding flexibly to a finite range of techniques infinitely varied in application. The trick is to listen inside the voice of the other and to resist bending it towards your own. All that's required is head-cracking concentration. In general, our writers tell us they like to crack heads. They appreciate productive resistance.

*

'You see/them shaved in the anthology.' That line floated free of a Michael Ondaatje poem and hooked in me. Hyperconscious of the Brick Books muchness that does not appear in this anthology, I want to think a little more about that shave. I had to leaf through *Rat Jelly* to find it in 'A Bad Taste,' one sentence in a family of sentences, one poem in a family of poems. Taking the line out of context shaves the poem thin – like representing each Brick Books writer with a single poem (no extra space for those we've published more than once) or letting a few general notes stand for editorial complexities.

Of course 'shaved in the anthology' does have a life of its own. 'Shaved' gives me shorn sheep or maybe a short-haired Samson or somebody spruced up by the barber. It gives me power tamed. If a book could speak, would it say (on its writer's behalf) 'Don't shave me'?

If it could be assumed that the common reader is an active collaborator in the making of meaning, one who can be trusted to understand the fragmentary nature of everything that reaches her in print, there would be no qualms about making anthologies. Anthology is a metaphor. Nothing contained is complete. There is always more, and you're not going to get it unless you rise up and hustle after it. Not even then, but at least you're up and moving. No reader of Brick Books (tell me I'm right about this) sits back and waits for the poem to come to her. Tell me also that, in consequence of their participatory natures, Brick Books readers cannot help but be good citizens.

*

I gathered choices of poems from the editors of Brick Books without a firm plan for making a Brick Books anthology. One possibility would have been to include half a dozen poems from each of, say, a third of our strongest writers. I wouldn't have enjoyed cutting anybody out, but quality is more important than inclusiveness. As I read through the material, though, I was gratified to find quality everywhere. So they're all here – every writer published by Brick Books over twenty-five years.

Of course we have been gearing up over those years. Three out of five poets on the 1999 Governor General's Award shortlist, and Jan Zwicky the winner – this is one public sign that we're doing our job well. Our poets have won their fair share of awards. But, for us, recognition takes the form of good poets asking us to publish them and good readers telling us they love the books.

*

One thing to notice as you read. Every one of these selections is *from* a volume, but the word 'from' (as in 'from *The Ledger*') is used only to sig-nify selection from a long poem or some other verbal fabric rent when a piece is torn off. Effort has been made to select intelligible and even self-contained pieces, but still…. As you will see for yourself, Brick Books is a poetry press that has occasionally opened out to other forms. Greg Curnoe submitted his *Deeds / Abstracts* to Brick Books, thinking of us as a publisher of his region because of our location in southwestern Ontario. We broke our mould to accommodate this fascinating 'diary' of five thousand years in the life of the plot of land that became Greg and Sheila Curnoe's home at 38 Weston St., London, Ontario. Of course before the mould was set we had published *Harrier*, a short story/chap-book by Terry Griggs. To follow the wonderful career of Terry Griggs, as you should, go to The Porcupine's Quill, which is also our much-esteemed printer.

*

If you were stubborn enough to read straight through to here, or if you've come here by jumping, I repeat my welcome. We wouldn't be much without readers. Without such excellent readers as we're proud to have attracted, we would have little to celebrate after twenty-five years. But with the help of real poetry readers I think we've done more than survive for all this time. I think we've done some good. This anniversary finds us occasionally exhausted but perpetually revived by the poetry that comes our way. Poetry is so good for you that a sizeable portion of the federal Health budget could profitably be diverted into it. I'm not kidding.

Stan Dragland and Don McKay (co-founders), with editors Sheila Deane (no longer active), Barry Dempster, John Donlan, Gary Draper, Clare Goulet, Marnie Parsons and Jan Zwicky. And with General Manager/Cheerleader Kitty Lewis, and Production Manager Sue Leclaire (succeeding Sue Schenk).

(Those interested in statements written to mark the occasion of our 20th anniversary, including a brief history of Brick Books, may find them and much else on our web site: www.brickbooks.ca)

*

Bert Almon

Constitutional

When I go running in the desert
over loose sand and packed sand
I'm thinking of very little
as the heart beats faster
lungs stretch tiny balloons

But when I sit down at the end
of the path, waiting for the pulse
to slow, the breath to slacken
I start thinking of many things

Inertia, for example: this running
is an affair of inertia, 'the effect
created by the totality of matter
distributed throughout the universe'

That has an empty sound
but it's everything there is
so that the distant stars
make their daily contribution
to my cardiovascular health
and I offer them freely
my own minuscule influence
over their dazzling cotillions
while pouring sand from my shoes

Earth Prime (1994)

Mia Anderson

Thaw

living on god time.
blink.
winter. blink. spring.
does it matter.
heigh ho another february song
only it's march.
ledge of ice slides under the river
like a pie knife.
spatula-coloured but for where
it still holds the dog up, flour edge and dry.
blink.
Dürer showing through the snow
in patches the look of Wit's
mane, the look of burdocks.
so what.
so heigh ho for god time.
march break.
wood ducks this year. they
break from the cedars and
circle the hermitage. good for them.
if love were all.
whereas. so much
remains undone. blink. the holes
of burrowing animals are busy with stain.
the barn isn't ready.
yesterday was like heaven, not wanting.
whereas.
to-day
          heigh ho the hermitage,
living on time.
slung on a break, and blinking.

Appetite (1988)

Les Arnold

the canvas bag

relax
it's a one
way
mirror
they can't

see
you & you
can't
see

Some Notes on the Paintings of Francis Bacon (1978)

Mike Barnes

Stirring a Can of Soup on the Stove

The windowpane is freckled with rain and I am
stirring a can of soup on the stove.
The thing, I think, is to do this;
just to do it, and only it. To remember perhaps
                as well
that this drizzling February afternoon will become
green-shooted April, then hot August,
in the comforting cliché of seasons.
To look no further, nor aim higher, than the opening
of this can of clam chowder, the addition
of a reasonable amount of milk
and the heating of both elements to an
edible warmth. Rye bread, icewater,
the hum of the fridge and there is some
cheese left if I am still hungry.

The rain taps, the element glows red, the darkness
                sets in.

As for the truly terrible events of the last
                two days
(which cannot be forgotten)
the thing, I think, is not to forget them,
but rather to remember that they happened, and
merely happened.
Neither to dismiss nor dwell upon
them, but to remember and heat this soup.
And then I think the thing to do is to
wash the dishes, set them up to dry,
make the bed as carefully as I ever have
and get into it.

Calm Jazz Sea (1996)

Rhonda Batchelor

Watching Birds
(for Marilyn Bowering)

she takes her binoculars &
books to roads outside
the town
past the geese
& fallen fences
& with the car
parked under green
shadows she walks into
woods alone
she hangs her sun hat on a
branch   her cardigan on
another   skirts the moss
covered logs   leaves
her shoes on a soft bed
of needles   wades through
shallow ferns until
she finds herself
in the focused light
of a clearing   exposed
at last

Bearings (1985)

Julie Berry

my lover's ex-neck and why

and why the hairdresser's giant purple nails
with square ends

why the soft
skin of my lover's ex-neck

and another thing
why the smoothness of the skin of my lover's ex-neck and the
squared-off ends of the hairdresser's giant purple finger-
nails and the trophies
the huge trophies in the in the huge
trophies in the shining in
the window

and why the purple nails the big purple nails
of the hairdresser

because the soft skin of my lover's ex-neck in his ex-car
because his wife rubs the feet of their palsied son and makes
aardvarks out of paper and water and glue

because my friend moans at the typewriter and tells stories
of two women who live together because she types with two
fingers and moans and says this is not and sighs working right
and the plastic virgin kneels on earl's chair hands folded
and because of water striders and raccoons and the curling
tendrils of my lover's ex-hair as it lies against his damp ex-
neck where i long to press my ex-lips remembering the moon and
the fire-pits when lake erie simmered and the world was smaller
than any word we settled on

worn thresholds (1995)

Guy Birchard

'I can be good company'

'I can be good company', Grey Owl
sighed
    where he had no company.

Anahareo's tenderness saves us
when we might fight; saves us
like the Bedouins, the Arab Lawrence led.

A woman on the c p line through Biscotasing
showed my brother old scars Archie gave her
with the point of his knife. She remembers him
talking to the wild.
He was not apostate;
he never was converted. Her eyes twinkle;
invite memory.

how to survive midwinter nights
with a single blanket, a lean-to
of boughs and a small fire? how to
stay alive all those hours?:

still my questions:
how to travel the rapids / by night
how to trap at all?

'I live for the small, 'live things.
They are my living, to whom
I credit my life. Their pelts
are worth more than yours and mine.
Still, Sir, I bow to you and, Madame,
I am charmed.'

Baby Grand (1979)

Walid Bitar

Sing Sing

The sun singed my tongue yesterday, so I'm
sticking out my neck

instead, sharpening my guillotine
shoulder blades, giving a piece

of my mind. Turn
the jukebox up! One little diamond

needle's vaccinating a whole
crowd against what

each of them might have done instead
of sitting out the week all over

town in the high-
rises,

the scaffolding from which the great outdoors
are slowly being

erased.
When it's all over I hope

they pencil in two of each
thing: two stones, two blades

of grass, two
trees, even two

people, one to sing
and listen, one

to look the other way.

Maps With Moving Parts (1988)

Marianne Bluger

The Treaties

Lady Simcoe to this hour
moves in grace among the savages
sheened in the glow of bonfires
set on the shore to fish salmon at night.
She watches them
from a high bluff.

When autumn comes she roams days long
under maples torched with fire
stepping lightly still
over leaf-lost trails
through a haze which is
the smoke of autumn mountains.

Even in winter her laughter rings out
from the bishop's palace at Québec
where great box stoves
are stoked to red heat for the ball.

Flushed she cries gaily
'Throw open the door.
There is just paper now –
a sheet of brown paper
between ourselves and hell.'

Gathering Wild (1987)

Robert Bringhurst

Jacob Singing
(for Roo Borson and Joseph Keller)

What I am I have stolen.
I have climbed the mountain with nothing in my hand
except the mountain. I have spoken to the god
with nothing in my hand except my other hand.
One against the other, the smith against the wizard,
I have watched them. I have watched them
wrestle one another to the ground.
I have watched my body carry my head around
like a lamp, looking for light among the broken stones.

What I am I have stolen.
Even the ingrained web
in the outstretched palm of this body,
limping on oracle-finger and thumb,
dragging a great weight, an arm or a tail
like the wake of a boat drug over the ground.
What I am I have stolen. Even my name.

My brother, I would touch you but these
are your hands. Yours, yours, though I call them
my own. My brother, I would hold your shoulders,
but only the voice is mine. My brother,
the head is a hand that does not open
and the face is full of claws.

What I am I have stolen.
These mountains which were never mine
year after year have remade me.
I have seen the sky coloured with laughter.
I have seen the rocks between the withered water
and the quaking light. I have climbed the mountain
with nothing in my hand except the handholds
as I came upon them, leaving my hands behind.

I have eaten the sun, it is my muscle,
eaten the moon, it is my bone.
I have listened to the wind, whipped
in the heart's cup, slap and whistle in the vein.

My father said:
the wood will crawl into the apple,
the root will crawl into the petal,
the limb will crawl into the sepal
and hide.
But the fruit has eaten the tree, has eaten the flower.
The body, which is flower and fruit together,
has swallowed its mother, root and stem.
The lungs are leaves and mine are golden.

I have seen the crow carry the moon
against the mountain.
I have seen the sky crawl under a stone.

I have seen my daughter
carried on the land's shoulder.
I have seen the wind change
colour above her.
I have lain in silence, my mouth to the ground.

I have seen the light drop
like a wagon-sprag in the crisp stubble.
I have seen the moon's wheels
jounce through the frozen ruts
and chirp against the pebbles.
I have seen the metal angels
clatter up and down.

I have seen the flushed ewes
churn in the pen and the picked rams boil
against the hazel. I have seen them
strip the poplar, scrub the buckeye bare.
I have seen the mixed flocks

flow through the scented hills like braided oil.
I who never moved as they do.
I have climbed the mountain
one foot up and one hoof down.

The breath is a bone the flesh comes loose around.

Flower and fruit together.
But this other, this other
who is always in the body,
lungs in the belly, head
between the thighs.
O his arms go
backward, his legs go
side to side.

My son, you have asked for a blessing. I give you
this blessing. I tell you,

the eye will flow out of the socket like water,
the ear will gore like a horn
and the tongue like another,
the sailor will stay in his house near the harbour,
the labourer, blinkered and fed, will stay at his labour,
the soldier will soldier,
the lawyer will smile like milk and swill liquor,
the judge will glide like a snake keeping pace with the horses,
the man with gay eyes will like chocolate,
the roebuck will wrestle the air and you will hear music,
the rancher will prosper,
the wolf will walk out of your hand and his teeth will be shining.

But this one, my grandson, the young one,
this one will steal
the sun and the moon, the eye and the tooth
of the mountain. This one will ride with his dogs
through the galleries of vision. This one will move
among the rain-worn shapes of men

with faces in his hands and the fingers writhing.
This one will slide his spade through the sea
and come away carrying wheat and linen.

This one, the young one, how tall,
shaking hands and trading armor
with his dark-eyed brother.

My son, you must do more
than listen to the angel; you must wrestle him.
And one thing further: he must be there.
The muscle in the air, the taut light
hinged in the milky gristle
and the swollen dark, the smell
like the smell of a cornered animal.

I have oiled these stones to sharpen the wind.
I have come or I have gone, I have forgotten.
I hold what I hold
in this chiasma of the hands.

I have set my ear against the stone
and heard it twirling.
I have set my teeth against the stone
and someone said he heard it singing.

from August Kleinzahler, ed. *News and Weather:
Seven Canadian Poets* (1982). This version from *The Calling:
Selected Poems 1970–1995* (McClelland and Stewart, 1995).

David Bromige

The poet

Society's the subject, you
the predicate. Call check
when you're to make that
presentation. Find those
citibank statements and read
the campus paper to be pleased
someone remembers the bismarck

Of course there's lots of ww 2 on pbs
Grainy corpses around stalingrad
who still perhaps believed
'I give my life for the fatherland
– i make a difference'
I for one enjoy arranging sounds
in the tradition of the text
whose need of tone
i respond to when alone
and happy, albeit sounding blue
not to be doing what i'm told to do

Tiny Courts in a world without scales (1991)

Colin Browne

The Holy Land

We are in another city.
The apple pie is not American.
The old poem is dead.

We are on a fluted edge above the ocean.
Someone listed as bride addresses the tripod.
Penetralia honoured & the lauded veil.

Pulverization of recent cellular fatalities.
Making the mast of it you might say gazing seaward.
Welcome aboard. Here's your T-shirt.

All this honey-coloured light!
These bushes rushing into flame!
Old stones. Yew!

A Menorah underfoot burns scarlet I swear it.
The lovers lead two pencils to radiant shrubs.
Singularly glandular or bargework.

We are on a word from *Swallows and Amazons*.
Names substitute for genital regions.
In the original she is an independent businesswoman in safety matches.

Precocity cited non-freezer vegetables and hasty insects.
Nutrition proved a spur to small automatic acts of kindness called breeding
                                              tactics.
We lay on the couch with your son to watch the great stars simulate breeding.

We might have bred right there, borne on interstellar particles of green
Neil Diamond was singing on the radio called over the sea.
We should have bred our fucking brains off.

Cucumbers incinerate, rendered spastically.

Dufy-boats smoke in the legs of fat girls trapped in waves.
We are in a city in a boy's mind and these are olive trees and
                                        that is the *Queen of Nanaimo.*

A cat sinks on the carport roof and interest rates jump down.
Streets of light in ruin on the former juvenile compound.
Boys aloft in their juniper with newspapers, women at the well at dusk.

Murmer of slippers.
Galilee.

Abraham (1987)

Julie Bruck

Timing Your Run
Philippe Laheurte (1957–1991)

The night before there was a break-in at your store.
There was an afternoon when the lock had been fixed,
and you said you'd drop an extra key at Laurent's place
after work. There was a call from your wife. All day,
you'd waited to run, but just as you went out,
it really started pouring. You were like a little boy
in the rain, Albert Mah said, and you came back drenched,
pleased with your time. There was a pair of New Balance
trainers for a customer with narrow feet, the rain
on the shoulders of the U P S man who waited
while you signed. A tuna sandwich made for you
at the dépanneur next door. Your thin fingers
on the brown paper bag. There was a blue car.
There was what you said about this run of bad luck –
robberies at the store, a fire on New Year's Day, about
training for a comeback in the fall, believing everything
could turn around. How happy the woman with long,
narrow feet was when you called to say her shoes
were in. There was your hand, hours after dark, slipping
the extra key through Laurent's mail slot, Laurent asleep.
There was a car coming. The key lay on the floor all night.
After running you'd showered in the store's tiny bathroom.
There was the bar of soap, still wet. There was a blue car
slicing a corner. There was your black car, stopped
at the light. There was Laurent, awake in the morning,
a freshly-cut key on the cool floor. There is tonight's
news footage of you winning races, explaining
the difference between two kinds of heel cups,
bending a shoe as you speak. There was the key
you wanted Laurent to have in case something
happened. There is Laurent, half-asleep, picking it up.

The Woman Downstairs (1993)

Anne Carson

Short Talk On Major And Minor

Major things are wind, evil, a good fighting horse, prepositions, inex-
haustible love, the way people choose their king. Minor things include
dirt, the names of schools of philosophy, mood and not having a mood,
the correct time. There are more major things than minor things overall,
yet there are more minor things than I have written here, but it is dis-
heartening to list them. When I think of you reading this I do not want
you to be taken captive, separated by a wire mesh lined with glass from
your life itself, like some Elektra.

Short Talks (1992)

Brian Charlton

after hours

Somewhere an ambulance sings too bad too bad too bad
and somewhere policecars flash you lose you lose
and somewhere a mother lullabies her children to sleep
while a husband is out on the town   even the typewriter
is part of it all   syncopation   music of the city after
hours   cosmic typewriter copcar cash register meatwagon
heavenly unlimited
                    cacasymphonious
                                        jazz

                    Not the symphony playing Beethoven in Victoria Park
                    Not the blues band at the York playing louder
                    Not the typewriter dear reader clack clackety
        clack   DING
a new line different than the one before
                    Not the pinball machine at the York Hotel

                                                        this
jazz is spherical pinball beginning at the centre and
pushing outwards to the city limits circling back on
itself beginning again the moment   it concludes

There is no finish to the city music   no start TOO
BAD TOO BAD YOU LOSE YOU LOSE YOU LOSE CLACKETY
                                        CLACKETY   DING
PINBALL CLACK

At the centre of space centre of the city all musicians
meet in one york hotel hole in the wall play taxicab
copcar freight train car crash blues all night too
bad you   Wait for that sublime when the HONK space   DING
music is pure   Sounds squeezed into Pinball rhythm and
beer glass mel-o-dee
                    ooEEE the jam never ends mother city

your musicians are mad
too bad you lose too bad you lose too bad you lose too

First ball

from *Angel & the Bear*
(the cosmic york hotel affair) (1979)

Hilary Clark

All Our Words Blow One Way

sun splashes sacraments over glass and ice, sharp wind and the immolation of desire. all our words blow one way, skittering. the frozen ground sings underfoot. breathless, we fly after weather-cocks spinning in wild, operatic gusts. this is how the work begins, in the mingled water and wine that pours glittering from water-sprouts, the sun on our bare heads. farce and sacrifice, our angelic nature clumsy, impure. buffoons brawl in the rowan tree, we should know, we've been there, punch drunk and crying out for grace

all our words lit from within. spirit rides a wave of annihilation, flirting, stung by desiring tongues. this is how the work begins, in the loving trickery of syllables, new wine effervescing, overflowing its cups. composing the fiery heart, fingers singed and winged. tipplers sing in the rowan tree, ecstatic, crying a new millennium.

More Light (1998)

Karen Connelly

I Kneel To Kiss The Ice

On a day grayer than a bitter sea
I return from the ocean.
My heart red and bitter
     as an ant, so obedient, so familiar,
     dragged by simple time into the habits of blood,
       twitching into and out of shadows,
       twitching to sister-skin,
         my body drawn like an insect
         to this sweet sick dirt.

I return to this country,
     so huge, but nothing grand.
The great trees here entomb me.
Snow angels haunt the air.
The plane burns down the runway
     long silver flame
     trembling.
Trembling, already I am up to my chin
in gravel and poplars, pines,
already surrounded.

The ghosts loom out of the snow
     like fantastic birds
       dancing
       all plume and pierce of talons
       striking, driving into skin,

touching, as lovers touch,
     or warriors in ancient battles,
     the way a murderer grasps weaker flesh

mothers touch their husbands,
who touch their daughters,
in turn, brothers, sisters,

those elaborate battles of small blood,
those memories of a dead dog
and a dead woman who left me
alone in the blue-green world
this white frozen world,
this country
trees, rocks, sky

and streets, the voice of my friend
in her attic of masks and paint:

>this is the city where something
>is always about to happen
>and never does –

streets I stumbled down
laughing, crying, the two words blur,
I dance down the pavement and my feet sting
I had to be born somewhere
I had to be born

the eternal surprise

and I am touched idiotically
by snow, the memory
of my five-year-old soul
believing deeply in diamonds
under the streetlights, blanketing
all the fields, the talcum of seraphs.

I come home
hating this language,
these words, my stories,
my eyes, hands, wishing
only to forget the clamour
inside that has brought me here
again

trolls sleep under
the pink bridge of my tongue

I kiss my mother's cheek
I reach to kiss the sky
Sticky pine sap is on my chin
I have been holding trees
I kiss the door of an old house

I slip down to the creek
on the edge of the city
and kneel to kiss the ice

my lip bleeds a little

I am not surprised.

This Brighter Prison: A Book of Journeys (1993)

Méira Cook

Light, moving

You had forgotten that words can be replaced, to begin
again is a point of honour. Like the beginning
of reading, how you spread honey on a page, as sweet
as this honey, so is learning. In the split light of noon
this city does not forgive us our trespasses.
Above the Alfama, the streets a contagion of light
and the opposite of light, somewhere the click of anklebone
on cobble.

This afternoon when we sat on the rim of the old city
sharing a pair of binoculars, a man many miles away
adjusted with terrible intimacy, his tv aerial.
During siesta, an hour opaque as forgiveness, all
water in the city pauses, resumes asynchronous.
I stop myself before I write, *houses fall like dice*
toward a sea as blue as a synonym (I was raised
a cubist, with a sense of astonishment) and bougainvillaea
caught *in flagrante delicto*. It is the beginning of the month
when gravity is strongest, climbing out of bed today
she stumbled but did not fall. In this heat our fingers
fatten subtly in the night so that rings
are awkward, mnemonic.

All day they watch tourists blot sun against thin skin
her shutter clicking amiably across the film she had forgotten
to replace, anticipating always the moment that precedes them
when they spill, glossy squares of colour from an envelope
slit by a wet forefinger. And Lisbon now,
smelt of green leather and diesel, the sour pout of dust
at the back of the throat. Wine, sharp olives, this day together

after an absence of years, the water, even the bread
salty with defections.

This is the sentence you write before you fall asleep
in the book that will later be lost somewhere between Madrid
and El Escorial: *only the animals defer to these curt*
afternoons, dogs lie where they fall in the squares
cats divide themselves from their shadows, and sleep
through siesta that lasts from the time it takes for light
to move across an open doorway, from left
to right, reading.

Toward a Catalogue of Falling (1996)

Marlene Cookshaw

It Happened in May, While My Sisters

navigated that corridor of treeless pasture.

I was with my husband. We were poking
our bills into morning-wet grass.

Something large enough to cast us both
in darkness shoved me to the ground.

My husband fled. There was no air
left in me, and I could not comprehend

the flash of the sun and the flash
of the sun cut off, again and at once.

Nor the senseless alarms of the chickens who
leapt sideways shrieking. The sun itself shrieked.

The shadow that rode me like a stone
from the great fir past the eucalyptus

bent a ray of the sun around me
in a thin gold blade that

pinned my breast to my shoulder.
What dropped, I know now, was a shadow

of the sun, elliptical because
it was morning. There are stories of this.

Lose your body in the grass,
stop your voice till shadows pass.

We see parings of this shadow sometimes,
very high up, and go to ground.

We lose our bodies in the grass,
we stop our voices till the shadows pass.

I shook off the shadow at the edge
of the honeysuckle, carried

the fragment of sun in my shoulder
under the spiked leaves of the Oregon grape.

The leaves opened my breath. The sun
went back to being above the trees.

I shoved deeper into the viny roots,
trying to shed what was left

of the brightness. Someone lifted me
into the light. I made myself shade.

Double Somersaults (1999)

Joan Crate

Gleichen

A wash-out ahead
so the train stopped for four days
on the prairie near Gleichen.
We played cards, told stories,
dined in Frogmore and St. Cloud.
Silverware, linen and china
chattered in our hands.
Like a picnic some said.

Then the Indians came,
Blackfoot, with their horses.
One dollar, their fingers sang, to ride
across the prairie and lick the sun.
Teeth glinted with sky.
But one pony fell in a badger hole
and broke its neck.
Look, said the man from Detroit,
the Indians will eat it.
They eat anything, diseased and
unclean things. Fingers pointed like
sticks of candy, laughter slapped.
The Blackfoot watched us, eyes bewildered
by sun. They rustled dry grass, vanished
into the yellow land smudge.

The gray horse bloated before us.

Pale as Real Ladies: Poems for Pauline Johnson (1989)

Michael Crummey

Rust

The boy watches his father's hands. The faint blue line of veins rivered across the backs, the knuckles like tiny furrowed hills on a plain. A moon rising at the tip of each finger.

Distance. Other worlds.

They have a history the boy knows nothing of, another life they have left behind. Twine knitted to mend the traps, the bodies of codfish opened with a blade, the red tangle of life pulled from their bellies. Motion and rhythms repeated to the point of thoughtlessness, map of a gone world etched into the unconscious life of his hands by daily necessities, the habits of generations.

On Saturday mornings the boy waits at the border of company property, rides figure 8s on his bicycle beside the railway tracks, watches the door beneath the deck head for his father coming off night shift.

Late September.

His father emerges from the mill in grey work clothes, a lunch tin cradled in the crook of one arm, his hands closeted in the pockets of a windbreaker. They head home together, past the concrete foundation of the Royal Stores that burned to the ground before the boy was born. Past the hospital, the hockey rink. The air smells of the near forest and sulphur from the ore mill and the early frost. What's left of summer is turning to rust in the leaves of birch and maple on the hills around the town, swathes of orange and coral like embers burning among the darkness of black spruce and fir.

The heat of their voices snagged in nets of white cloud. Their words flickering beneath the surface of what will be remembered, gone from the boy's head before they reach the front door of the house on Jackson Street. The mine will close, the town will collapse around them like a building hollowed by flame.

It will be years still before the boy thinks to ask his father about that other life, the world his hands carry with them like a barely discernible tattoo. His body hasn't been touched yet by the sad, particular beauty of things passing, of things about to be lost for good. Time's dark, indelible scar.

Hard Light (1998)   45

Greg Curnoe

What We Live On

Today, Sunday, February 9, I was skiing down the back with our dogs. By skiing along the old river bed I have been able to get around the huge piles of snow dumped by the city. While going this way I am able to look up at the old river bank that forms the north boundary for all the lots on Weston Street. I realize that I am looking at a landscape not very different from that seen by Augustus Jones when he surveyed the river in January and February 1793. Probably the view from the flats is not that different in some respects to what it was when there was an Iroquoian camp some hundreds of years ago at the intersection of Foxbar Creek and the old river bed. In the woods at the foot of the old river bed there are the mounds of incinerator ash from Victoria Hospital medical waste that May Abrams walked through when she was a child in the 1920's. She has told me how frightening it was walking through the still smouldering piles at night. As I skiied further east I tried to visualize the fields of vegetables and flowers that the Bartlett family grew on the flats in the 1860's. I passed the old road that is still used as a path from Weston Street to the river. This is the road that Ernie Potter talks about that was used by the gardeners to get their produce up the hill. On the top of the hill they had orchards. I thought about the Moravians rafting back to Moraviantown along here, as they headed back to their ruined village in 1814. It had been burned by the Americans in the aftermath of the Battle of Moraviantown. As I look around my mind is filled with images of people and things who have occupied this area and I can see the landscape which consists of willows, frozen ponds and a steep hillside with backyards along the top. The earth moves enough to disrupt surveyors stakes, that is it moves in detail but stays the same in its over-all appearance.

Because the area behind us is wild and overgrown, it is timeless. But there is the story of the retired British Army engineer, General William Renwick, who owned in the 1870's what was called the tongue of land that extended south from what is now Nelson Street. At that time the river still curved south so that the water's edge formed the north boundary of our lot. What remains now is a series of long ponds, actually they are identical to the coves only smaller, because the General caused the river to change its course. Apparently he dug a ditch across the tongue of land, about where the river flows now. When the great flood of July 1883 struck it gouged out a new channel where the General's ditch was. In doing so it did a lot of damage to Henry Winnett's house (which was on high land at the east end of Front Street) in addition to destroying four new cottages and washing away six acres of land on the river flats. General Renwick lost an expensive law suit for damages to Winnett's property.

Yesterday, February 8, the dogs were barking at a man and a boy who were getting water from an open spot in the old river in a blue plastic drum. They were using it to flood the frozen section east of us. They are doing what generations of residents of Weston Street have done, exploring the woods down the back, skating on the frozen river bed, making dug outs and shacks and so on. The street and its goings-on are probably typical of areas of the city near the river. My sons Owen and Galen and Mark Favro made a terrific video tape of an explosion of fireworks in one of the four-foot-high concrete storm sewer pipes down the back. There is this brilliant rolling ball of fire with smoke coming out of the pipe. Owen was talked out of shooting it from the inside. A few years ago someone built a birdwatching blind on a small island in the old river bed just east of us. My kids saw the bird watcher occasionally.

I can remember when they were digging the foundation for the Harper's house next door last summer, seeing the layers of rubble then the sandy topsoil profile of the original river bank and the light grey clay below that. That was my first realization of what we actually live on.

Deeds / Abstracts (1995)

Lynn Davies

Lord, if You Had a Lap

Lord, if you had a lap, I'd sit on it tonight.
I'd tell you how my hurting songs have come true
at last. My speaking voice stuck
as my singing sounds on those 2,000
newly pressed records from Toronto.
Every single one of them skipping
to repeat my lines, sure as Lela Bennett's
dog's tail used to thump the kitchen floor
when I walked in her back door
for beer and sweet rolls. Lord, hear my voice,
broken as the next shipment of records
I poured like cornflakes from boxes
marked 'fragile'. To get away, Lela and I
rode the Yarrnouth-Bar-Harbour ferry in March,
rode a storm that drove all those big truck drivers
out of the lounge, their hands held over their mouths
to catch their insides boiling over. Just me
and Lela left to share fried smelts and potatoes,
watch the curtains swing as if that gale roared
through the dining room. And every time that boat reared
then fell, to meet the ocean,
her metal buzzed like an out-of-tune loose string
on my guitar. You heard me then, Lord,
thanking you for boats that stay upright,
good food and patience. It took them two hours
to chip the ice from the ferry doors
so we could drive my old Ford Fairlane south
under trees wearing flowers all pink and white
and brighter than any sequinned shirt I ever wore.

It's there I told Lela she carried for me
more melody than I could ever write.
I thought she heard me then and I thought
she heard me since, but this spring back home

she found a man loving his saxophone
and her watching him while he plays bars
with a back-up band spinning tunes
I couldn't copy if I tried.

Leaving me to write new songs
on a pile of empties growing fast
as the good lines keep coming.
Lord, could I pop you a beer to celebrate
those 2,000 broken records remade
into tapes small enough to navigate this world's
great fickle current before freeze-up.
But Lord, will anyone hear me this time?

The Bridge That Carries the Road (1999)

David White, *Peggy Dragišić,* Patrick Deane, *Sheila McColm*

Speak softly

Speak softly, winter
these words in the warm
wing-tufted meaning:
let a sparrow alight on the line.

Face of Grace is
Winter. This year. This once. This Again.
Consolation   is: her Mildness,
Saying: 'Poor trying world. I go you gently   /   To warming.'

Africa asking
            What's Winter?
shivers at this consolation.
Grace into wildness breaks.

When the pattern permits all possibilities
occur, cohere. The voices, responses, questions
of all times and climates and continents
take hands like Botticelli's ladies in the leaves.

from *Renga** (1980)

---

* The Renga is originally Japanese, a collaborative form, a sòrt of round robin
  in which stanzas are composed by each poet, passed to another and so on until
  a poem is completed. To the four sections of four poems so produced, like
  the one above, were added a fifth four-quatrain poem wholly written by each
  poet.

Barry Dempster

Books Are

Books do not breathe, or
share your soup, stroke your
arms, inhale your rare perfumes.
Books do not spit, love or scheme
for more. Books do not live
parallel lives. Books do not
pray or hold mirrors unto God.
Books do not die with regrets.

What books do is talk
endlessly. Not to you or
the sycamores or the china
cups, but to no avail at all.
Talk, more talk. Books have
something to say and are bound
to say it. Books equal
their words exactly.

Since my last letter I have
been a book or several books
together. I do not listen
or spit. I talk to thin air.

Books are and emphasize.
Nothing, they chant and storm
will ever stay the same. The
wind on everything, pages
turned, pages torn.

Letters From a Long Illness With the World:
The D.H. Lawrence Poems (1993)

John Donlan

Buffalo Jump

I'm here to get loaded, not lucky
cresting the lines of beautiful youth at the bar.
Cute guys, dream cars – Arthur Rimbaud,
you've got a lot to answer for.

Bang, bang, bang, bang. That'll do me.
Homing: mallards' voices guide each other
across the dark water, safe to the gravel bar.
The court house, the Bell building, the moon.

We stood under the little dam in Baysville
wearing the river, each in our wet world.
School, work: in the belly of the whale,
weekends free for domestic economy and

for that we have cast in our lot together
turn up the amp, Pointed Sticks, DOA,
Doppler Effect, Teenage Head, Sheep Look Up,
let our pure anthem pour over us.

Domestic Economy (1990)

Peggy Dragišić

this is to be

ahhh …
this is to be pregnant with sun,
every limb fruit-full
satisfied heavy
this is to be golden,
not Midas metal but
apricot
taut and tender stuffed
with light

I have harvest babies
apricot burnished babies
russet apple gleaming chestnut
babies
winter-sown
summer-grown
harvest babies

optimistic babies
in disregard of brunette genes
to come out so copper
coloured
as if to say
Mom mind's gloom's
quite absent in body's womb
there, Mom, it's
all sun

four eyes across the picnic
table
all blue
two round bad and merry
two long in tangled shadows
two noses, mouths, four ears,

legs, arms, twenty
fingers! twenty
toes!
beyond all arithmetic
love-stuffed cells
of aweful life
uncountable

from *From The Medley* (1978)

Marilyn Dumont

Leather and Naugahayde

So, I'm having coffee with this treaty guy from up north and we're laughing at how crazy 'the mooniyaw' are in the city and the conversation comes around to where I'm from, as it does in underground languages, in the oblique way it does to find out someone's status without actually asking, and knowing this, I say I'm Metis like it's an apology and he says, 'mmh,' like he forgives me, like he's got a big heart and mine's pumping diluted blood and his voice has sounded well-fed up till this point, but now it goes thin like he's across the room taking another look and when he returns he's got 'this look,' that says he's leather and I'm naughahyde.

A Really Good Brown Girl (1996)

E.F. Dyck

Introduction

Consider my cat Jack:
He has sight in one eye,
He has lost both his tanks,
He has sired three kittens,
He pisses on the four elements,
On his throat a faint star
Shows: his breed is not perfect.
Otherwise, he is grey all grey.
Consider, now, Jack's master:
I own him, his body, his soul.
Otherwise, my sight is perfect,
My son or my daughter is gone,
I prefer my numbers prime,
And my hair, too, is grey.

from *Pisscat Songs* (1983)

Patrick Friesen

I'll say whatever you want

I'll say whatever you want that the river is rolling with heads I'll say I've haunted highways with a blade I've sliced a fetus from its womb and nailed a lizard to a tree I've lived in doorways heard lovers through the walls I'll say whatever you want and it's the truth I'll say whatever you want there are no fingerprints

I am the phone call you dread the filthy words the pain you hide behind your pills I am your mother with her guilt your father with his amnesia

I am your divinity the monster you dream at night I am who you want to be free with a pocketful of gold I am your leader I speak from the throne

this is not a confession this is a treatise on love this is your religion your philosophy of life this is how you make truth

I will tell you who I am I will tell you who you are

from *A Broken Bowl* (1997)

Cherie Geauvreau

vocation

once when I opened my mother's door a crucifix of steel
pierced my right hand. fallen, flown, it had buried itself in
bone, a spear ashine in the cap of golgotha.

I wept. I was moved by the flinty crown and silver feet. the
ache and shame like sweet pulp in his disfigured face. I grew
my skin to wrap him, warm him in living flesh.

I bore him to table but no one saw as I drank cups and cups
of madness in red.

mother twisted away. father was trapped in song, I waved my
christ uselessly over the melody. I knelt beneath my
brother's fist and offered the cross to him. he mocked this
new deformity, this sin so great.

the left hand began to do everything: to cover the mouth, the
eye, the vulva. the left hand (Verso), closest to the heart,
grew and grew. the right hand (Jesus), planted in bloodstone,
averted death forever. amaranth.

Even the Fawn Has Wings (1994)

Susan Goyette

The moon on Friday night

erased all paths to Saturday
and swept up footsteps from the day before. It coaxed buttons
to the lips of buttonholes and whispered, 'you're beautiful,
so beautiful,' to women who speak the vernacular

of loneliness. Softly it slid into the hands of the men
they were with and lent its light to everything they touched.
'See,' the moonlight seemed to say, 'there are so many ways
to be naked and so many ways to be far

from home.' The light reminded the women of songs
they knew, songs written to gauge distance. Later,
still later on this island of Friday night, they sang
those songs under their breath as they bent

to tie their shoes. And they stayed bent long after
their shoes were tied, hearing the wind for the first time
caught in a bucket of baby teeth. It was then they remembered
they were toothfairies, medicine men, and their children's

mouths were empty. They knew of light switches, window
blinds, they knew to throw sand on fire, to blow
at a candle, but this light, this light they knew nothing
about so they carried it home with them. And now they wish

they hadn't. It lights up corners they'd kept dark, lights
their words and gives them new meaning. At night,
they hold their husbands' hands to their mouths
'Know this light,' they pray, 'touch me with this light.'

The True Names of Birds (1998)

Neile Graham

Sea Glass From Execution Rock

This is the gift my mother gives –
a hint of vision, chunk of glass
tongued and ground by waves,

tossed onto the rock by
winter tides. This
my mother sees; having walked

across the mudflats to the remains
of Ohiat village to Execution Rock,
she finds this bit of green

with the taste of ocean, some white
man's bottle turned into beauty
by sand and time.

Another gift, the tale of her journey.
She writes *Last night was special dark,*
dark with all possible stars,

the milky way and quiet.
We were out in a herring skiff
admiring bioluminescence trailing

from paddles and dip nets....
Stars above and below!
I told her I'd steal those words

to trade for what I cannot see
in the city except a hint that rides
in with winds from the Sound, a rumour

that brings the ocean here.
The cedars outside my door shake it for news,
and I stand outside in dim winter rain

on my way to work, guess at the meaning
of the weaving branches, the taste
of salt air, touch the bit of glass

in my pocket to see the cloud-hidden stars,
the falling rain catching sparks from streetlights
to scatter on the streets below.

Spells for Clear Vision (1994)

Terry Griggs

There was a dead man

There was a dead man in Uist who wouldn't stay buried. Six times they buried him, deeper each time, and six times his coffin floated to the surface of the ground, as if earth was water. The seventh time they buried him they asked his lover, for whom he had slain himself, to sit by the grave. When the coffin floated again to the surface, the woman opened it, and a great bird, some kind of a hawk, flew out and landed on her shoulder.

What the river flowing from my grandmother brings. Him. He stepped into her dreams and swam down to me. Now he's the current, the sinew, the stinging whip in my own dreams. I can almost see him. A shadow in the doorway. Years after she had given him up he still came to her night after night. Still offered the same gold ring. My mother and I both wear one like it. Where'd you steal that, she asks, from your wife? I found it, in a lady's slipper. You're daft, she says. Will you wear it, Jeannie, will you wear it? 'No,' my mother screams. Nightmares again. I have them as' well. He hounds me. Follows me, relentlessly, always getting closer and closer. What was it last night? I ask my mother. Cats clawing at my throat, she says offhandedly. And you? Some man, I couldn't see his face. He either wanted to give me something or kill me, I'm not sure which.

from *Harrier* (1982)

Don Gutteridge

Cornering

1

When we were young
we cornered as the
wind and windward
went down

snow-packed bicycle paths
drew us under the
ribbed Bridge with
quicksand / questions

thru October cattails
blown and ragged
milkweed morning

past the river-bank
and summer under
water seldom seen
(thunder dreamed)

beyond the smoking docks
the reeking fisheries

over c.n. tracks and out
to fields sweet
with manure

past the Slip and on
to Canatara:
the great Lady mirroring
sky and village
galaxies of sea-beasts
no wind ever blew upon

(when the sun falters
they crawl on our
shivering beach)
and back
thru wet clover
ploughed fields
First Bush
first blinking still-wet
dawnlight drew us
cycling
       home.

2

When we were young
we covered the four
corners of our village
but never found them:
only
       a breeze turning
       a bridge beginning
       a road too straight
for the multicycling wind
for the wheels under
              and in us.

God's Geography (1982)

Naomi Guttman

Reasons for Winter

I   Persephone

Mother, it's not as they say:
while your back was turned I prayed
for the ground to open
and the arm that took me down

was solid. The fruit his wet hand slit
– those tart red bombs he fed me –
converted me, their intelligence
so palpable I felt the sun in my throat.

II   Demeter

After you vanished the sky
stayed blue, the fields unaltered,
but my mouth was a husk, my hands
a fever. Sheaf within my sheaf,
my single blond kernel, my skin
is helpless without you.

O earth, once teeming in my care, somewhere
you opened your muddy lips and drank her.
Until I know that chimney of loss
I will not trust you anywhere.

Reasons for Winter (1991)

Phil Hall

yellow canoe

(yellowed brush/ feta dipped in Bushmills)

at the end
he said "Put in my canoe
(unfreighted & never wet)
the following provisions

my two volume Lives of the Poets by Johnson

my tenor banjo (ivory pegs)   ...

my 16-gauge
& the toy cannon from Edinburgh Castle
        D'Arcy lost on the train to Aberdeen

full of nectarines my blue & white bowl
& dully pink my tin half-litre carafe

my custodianship of raindrops 350,000,000 years old
        fossildrops around tracks in stone

        (the 3-toed Mother-Of-Us-All
        loping through bog-downpour
        into rockhound/midwife arms)

'It's A Wonderful Life' (uncolourized)

my photo of Simone Weil
        — the one I wrote 'to Phil with love' beneath

the time Lawrence & I walked under Vancouver
        through the tunnel of muck dug for the coming subway

my Bullfinch's Mythology (Casa Loma gift shop)

my hoya – toward the day it ever blooms
        velvet stars dripping honey!

our flight over the Parthenon
        in a NATO 19-seater bucking
        & Brett asleep in my arms

my 37-pound muskie (ambitious/ prone)

not just any golf club / guitar – essential it be
        the fretted 2-iron shown to me near –
(none of this may still exist)   ...

my 'ultra/ left' button
        my silver horse-&-saddle pin
        my 'make poetry useful' button

my beaded string-tie from Manitoulin Island

*the marginoclastic **Collected Poems** of D.H. Lawrence*

the fox I met in the snowfall at the cow-pond

my bodhran
        & my debts nipped with a shrug

my beanbag moonman

Acushla Acushla Acushla ...

& my glasses

but throw my ashes after me
off Little Bob Bridge

suspend my readied canoe
from a blue ceiling
(neither a private collector's nor municipal)

& ripple your hands as you pass under ...”

so ripple your hands as you pass under
his haberdash-catafalque pointed both ways

& read a quote painted where a name might have been
if he hadn't thought names were whitecaps in vaults:

'Sleep! In your boat brought into the living-room
supreme admirer of the ancient sea'

from *Hearthedral: a Folk Hermetic* (1996)

J.A. Hamilton

Barbara's Garden
(for Sandy)

We sat at a restaurant table in 1985
talking of women, of men, of Barbara.
I wanted to move your hand to my lips,
quietly, the smallest of gestures.
It was very beautiful that night: the sky
above Stanley Park freckled with stars,
the candles on our table unwavering.
You spoke of passion, the desire in this world
to make, to stand, to accomplish: how we are counted.
Your mouth was an instrument of great love.

Now I imagine Barbara in her garden:
each spring she lifted the season into light,
turning it to examine corners and mirrors,
its tucked away pulse, listening for the vibration of life.
Barbara at her typewriter, her articulate fight
through the thicket of the body, slashing and burning:
What is wisdom? What is flesh?

You who held this woman in your arms, who laughed
with her, who soothed her sore, troubled passage
know this: her answers were small.
She was the first to speak of time
cut off at the knees, the breasts, tongues.
Later you bent to the necessary tasks,
set your house running, the ragged whir and tick
after Barbara, counting the breaths of your solitude.

You moved through rooms unlocking cabinets and
file drawers, lifting carpets. You opened windows.
You stood in the rain but it was cold.
Your body had ears and eyes, it told the truth.
Waking, not certain it was waking. In Barbara's garden
your hasp of hunger opened, closed, opened.

Steam-Cleaning Love (1993)

Maureen Harris

The Mother of Us All

wiped her forehead
Cain's nose
Abel's face
Seth's bottom
pitched the boys outside
to play in the farmyard.

She yelled at her no-name daughters
to quit messing in the dirt
and go tidy their rooms.
Cursed Adam
gone to town
three days now.

The mother of us all
leaned against her tree, sighed
for the snake, his green quiver,
his sibilant caress, his
supple tongue that promised
a different Paradise.

A Possible Landscape (1993)

Brian Henderson

If language is not strange

If language is not strange to itself
how can it be its own?

A word is a hunger, a power spot
like a body, a sea

flooding itself with fish, sown
with currents, glimmers

Beyond its margins palms wave

Deep in the ground
it pulls minerals from rocks
and listens to the talk of fossils

is given
gills, feathers, fire, palm fronds
spun with the silk of memory

and when we are re-
membered through its shimmering, alien
depths, we can listen with our skins

The heart that flutters there is
almost heard

overheard

over the wash of sea-pull
womb-beat: the wings

of a hairstreak

Year Zero (1995)

Cornelia Hoogland

A Woman's Strength
Eppie Hoogland

The moment the cornered rat reared
on its haunches, teeth bared,
was the moment his mother lunged
her spear-body
into the round spear-handle
of the broom and the rat screamed
and blood leapt up at her;
it was as if she tore
through the safe crook of her father's arm,
her village on the Wieregen Mere,
her shyness with the Frisian boy
in hiding from the Germans,
her too-accomplished sister,
the slights and put-downs; as if she
had stalked the Atlantic, cracked the shield,
the prairies, all of Canada beneath
her bloody knees and hands to get
into this moment.

Not an unkind mother, but
she didn't comfort the horrified kids
then or ever, as if this way they could better learn
the new country. The eldest child, my husband,
stayed to watch her flick the rat onto newspaper,
then scrub the blood from the chair legs, the walls,
her bare knuckles in the bucket of pink water,
that woman on all fours, her heavy breasts and haunches
gleaming like the purple heart in a bag of skin
when you crack open an egg.

Sometimes when he kneels behind me
lifts my belly so my arms straighten

and my knees bend and he enters
I know he is only as far away as a cougar
is from the deer it tracks,
but just at the moment the animals
skid to a halt he clamps my breasts
into his hands, pushes them up through
my body as if to plaster his own hollow chest;
claiming and fearing
what a cornered woman is capable of.

Marrying the Animals (1995)

Helen Humphreys

Reunion

I've forgotten more faces than I remember, and everyone's
changed or isn't. The flutter of arbitrary deaths and marriages.

The past stays where it was, that's the deal. Time a shining
ring. Nebula. Marry me. Because I said so. Because it seems

I was the only one seriously necking with the
high school janitor. He was old then, is dead now,

and I'm not sorry for anything. It's a surprise
to still have those kisses, to know my body has been more

faithful than my mind. And I wouldn't have guessed or
wanted that. The press of his chest on mine, sprung camber

of ribs. Grey beard soft on my open mouth. I could feel
his breathing, can feel it now, that particular arch

and fall, how one person's breathing is unlike another's, how
the rhythm of the body sways time and language, moves us out

of our lives and back into them. And I know this now,
only. Let your body remember what it was sure of. We only have

this long. Get it right. Press your ear to these lines, the memory
of me, over here by the furnace in the boiler room, breathing.

Anthem (1999)

Francis Itani

The Photo (ii)

In the Rowboat

That summer season we were:
sisters, brothers, a dog –
black and white, sentinel of the prow.
The boat wore its spring coat of paint
(every year the same forest green)
soaked in shallow waters after each winter
till the wood swelled and sealed.
Father, pleased, stalked the shore
scanning the wide swift waves.

Now we are in the boat:
Father, long neck stretched, turns
to shore, oars poised over water.
Five children, you between two small brothers
in the stern; an arm round each,
every angle, every contour clear.

Now, beneath the waves
the image mirrors children underwater.
Faces blur, recover the surface;
Father's neck ripples to distortion.
The oars bend, trapped
in deep-locked wells.

A Season of Mourning (1988)

A.R. Kazuk

I: My Home Is Opened Space

Sit, settle back! Watch a movie with me. We've seen these telescapes in
so many variants we already know the hero like a brother.
A stream of images behind the scrolling
credits, Tull's early life,
flashes by …

A boy's territory	My home opened space, door-frames my place.
extending beyond	Billowing sheers and the table-legs.
the oven's	My coat with an orange stripe on the sleeves.
glowing thing	The sodden yard alive with lava after rain
	more private than a dream.

cutting to	Unities of deer and headlights at times
the shadowlands	slowed traffic on the town's inroads,
between bush	under pines heavy with weight of snow
and yard,	wakeful as babies teething.

two pots	My shadow, bent on fences,
and a kettle,	honey passer-by has touched
	with her small black shoe
	and bobby socks,
	but did not break.
	Across my mouth, a bit of mica,
	the grin-flake.
	Stove-pipe my jeans:
	new kittens
	under my toque.

that moment before	Her strikes hit my hands precisely,
first love,	so that I cannot hold a ball of string.
	The kite falls, an iron bell.
	Tomorrow, maybe
	the United Nations will intervene.

places where   The metallic bees in the young vine,
the father   gulls winded on muddy lawns,
might have been   have come too late to interest me.
  In high, deep branches there is a tavern
  the magpie keeps
  where I spend my time.

Cowardice   To have never kissed you
on love's terms.   bothers me tonight
  as I put this down slowly,
  my lips borrowing on this credit:
  never to have kissed you.

Places where   Overcast has ripped open a letter, sun garnishees
even the knees   the rain's belly, and school-girls have formed
of young girls   a long ellipsis with their regulation black umbrellas.
turn to gold.   The breeze positions sparrows
  along eaves around the Bank of Commerce.

The stream drifts   I am as I have always been, strangeness,
to Tull's uncle,   ant-hills and sticks articulated once
Horace Waters,   and which the dolphin-songs could not absolve,
speaking   though simian chests have shed hair. Order
in a mirror,   disseminates among my microphones,
  swift-dreaming indeed as the ionosphere!

receiving   Marooned upon my generosity's reefs,
his sister,   tall and jewelly even now
Tull's mother,   like a monthly magazine. It's time
in his office,   she inserted her concern for the boy,
  into my lapel
  like an Easter Island head.

and finally	Khaki clay drank quarts of black blood;
to a boy fishing	sunglint on warm blade: I saw
with a book	Gouvernail in my uncle's smile.
on a Sunday,	A ribbon drawn bright from its dossier,
	when he showed me how to peel roe
	from a salmon's cold salute.

and a cabin,	Thrifty and not understandable, through the door
violets overgrown.	I hear horses bringing near the distance.
	I wonder how frightful I will be
	to the verandah blushing in that widening slit.

While the commercials
    are on let's talk about
        new, fresh and free, the trinity of our time. The Father,
            the Son and the Holy Ghost. Liberté, Egalité, Fraternité.
        New and improved, the history of religions, Higher Criticism,
Eighteenth-century grammars, Puritan lace.... We're responsible for
this layering don't you think? Right, and for an archaeology of deceit.

from *Microphones* (1987)

Janice Kulyk Keefer

Meeting by Water

Out of this maze of streets a stranger walks toward me.
Unpremeditated yet expected, he has perfect manners
and a pair of wings, dwarfed, misshapen,
clotting the place where his heart should be.

Together we walk to a bridge over a great river.
We do not cross but stand looking down
at the drifting boats, at streetlamps sunk
like eclipsed moons.

I open my coat and show him my birthmark:
a wattled stain, coloured like blood stirred
into mud. He puts his mouth to my breasts;
the stain is wine, pours clear away.

When I touch them, his wings become wishbones,
break apart. Now there is nothing between us.
We stay on the bridge a long time,
arms round one another, eyes closed

as the river rises. It carries us off,
together, in different directions.
Everything solid has vanished.
The air fills with a smoke like rain.

Marrying the Sea (1998)

Michael Kenyon

Rice

My daughter does this funny thing with her hands when she sees Dave or me after she's not seen us for a while. Dave calls it a microwave because it's fast and almost no movement at all. She keeps her arms stiff at her sides, darts the fingers of both hands quickly away from her body, then back. A tiny swimming motion. A long distance hug. Her eyes showing how happy she is.

I take her to the library and sit her looking at picture books in the children's section. The library's a good place to begin, if you have the time to read. You need a library card and people are nice and helpful. Dave says there are as many murders in the library as on TV[, just as many awful things as in the newspaper. He's wrong, there's worse. But I get more afraid in The Brick, buying appliances, than I get by my daughter's side reading horror in articles and books. Nobody tries to snow me, or sell me stuff. I look at her microwave and want to know every terrible thing going on in the world, and if it gets real bad I can always close my book, look over her shoulder into the same old forest.

Rack of Lamb (1991)

Don Kerr

that man knew

that man knew Berryman
and this man Yeats
would you be willing to be interviewed?
they say and I say wait
till we've met someone
everyone knows is first rate
and they say who?
well in Montreal there's
someone met Cohen
and the coast thinks the gulf stream's
the main stream but the great plain
is next door to the great plain
and our metropolitan areas
are secondary and tertiary at best
it is the role of the margin
to be marginalized
the role of the hinterland
to hint
          in lower case
          our only caps
are baseball caps
farm machinery caps
or twist off caps

this woman knew Lowell
and that woman Larkin
now I got a list but I'm loyal
I'm taciturn
a plain man
it's the role of the uncanonized
not to provoke the gods
to be the anon of canon
let others be the small bore

but for goodness sake
what of w & r & b & k
well I'd say
it's too early to tell

Autodidactic (1997)

Lyn King

Night Speaks

This is what I want when I want
perfectly. When desire is a sleek
animal bred for cold. Night

speaks coyote, native tongue
of the mountains. Long
howls thrown like safety ropes
from one peak to another. Listen

with the body. What
sounds the ear refuses
the blood accepts and translates
in the brain. That howl means
lonely runs unchecked
through veins through heart   snags
on the V in the throat.

This howl means want means
yearn means both these
mated. Their off-spring a
small gnat dug in, burrowing.

Sleep, in the mountains,
is never empty. Coyotes
tear through it in waking
packs. What dream
could sound like
this, have me wishing

to be this one or this one
who sings his heart
in one long note? The call
of exempt things

all but the raw smell curled
into some fallen leaves. Fur, blood,
the sound footfall looses
into the baffle of earth.

That one note, its pitch the cracking
that empties night. The sound
a soul makes thrown against the sky.
In some it comes up through dreams
like air through water. In others
it rears. Is felt in the fingernails,
the teeth. That lone note is the history
of singing. The reason mouths grope
like hands around the air.

The Pre-Geography of Snow (1987)

Robert Kroetsch

'the nether millstone'

> They were draining the pond to do some work on
> the dam. Seeing a few fish at the floodgate, Henry
> sent one of his sons for a bucket. The boy, stepping
> into the water, catching fish with his bare hands,
> filled the bucket. Henry could hardly believe his
> eyes. But he sent the boy for a sack. And couldn't
> believe. But sent the boy for a tub, for a barrel.

Joe Hauck got his arm caught in the water wheel.
He screamed. But no one heard him.

He couldn't get free. The wheel was trying to
lift him up to heaven. He couldn't get free.

Joe Hauck had a good head on his shoulders, a
cap on his head. He threw his cap into the racing

water. The men unloading logs below the mill
noticed the cap; they ran on up to the millsite.

The doctor had good horses; he got there that same
day. Three men held Joe Hauck flat on a table,

right next to a saw, while the doctor patched
and sewed, ran out of thread, broke a needle.

to
chopping
8
bags

.40

you must see
the confusion again
the chaos   again
the original forest

under the turning wheel
the ripened wheat, the
razed forest, the wrung
man: the nether stone

page 117: Paul Willie

1893:

by 1/2 Day Work	.38
" work with team	2.00
" 100 lbs of flour	.85
" 25 bushels lime	3.12
" plowing potato patch	1.50
" working at dam	2.00
Team to Mildmay	.50
by 5 cord of wood	8.00
" beef 87 lbs at 5 ¢	4.35
" hay 1,000 lbs	4.00
" 2 hemlock logs	.75
" 1-20 ft cedar log	.50
" 3-16 ft cedar	.75

it doesn't balance

1854 to 1910:

to sawing Butternut
"   "   Pine
"   "   Basswood
"   "   Birch
"   "   Soft Elm
"   "   Rock Elm
"   "   Cedar
"   "   Tamarack
"   "   Maple
"   "   Beech
"   "   Black Ash
"   "   Hemlock
"   "   Cherry

it doesn't balance

The bottom of the pond was not so much mud as fish. The receding water was a wide fountain of leaping fish; Henry sent a daughter to go fetch Charlie Reinhart, Ignatz Kiefer, James Darling, Peter Brick. The neighbours began to arrive (and strangers, bearing empty sacks) from up the road to Formosa, from down the road to Belmore; the neighbours came with tubs and barrels, with a wagon box, and they clubbed at the eels that skated on the bright mud. They lunged at the leaping trout. They pounced like bullfrogs after bullfrogs. And they swam in the quick, receding flood.

the grinding stone
that does not
turn:

under the turning
stone: the nether
stone: the ledger

intending to stay

> The children screamed after their leaping, swim-
> ming parents. They didn't believe their eyes. They
> bathed in the clean, the original mud. They flung the
> fish onto dry land and themselves stayed in the
> water: they usurped the fish. The floodgate was
> open, the dam no longer a dam. They rose, blue-
> eyed and shouting, out of the tripping, slippery
> mud: while the fish, their quick gills strange to the
> sudden air, drowned for lack of water.

the children, sitting hunched on the dam,
hearing Joe Hauck scream, were silent.

In all their lives they had never heard Joe Hauck
scream (his arm mangled: by the turning wheel).

People said Joe Hauck was never the same

after that water wheel tried lifting him

up to heaven. No matter what he did, people shook
their heads. 'He's not the same,' they said.

When his brothers went west to homestead, Joe
elected to stay at the mill. He wasn't the same.

from *The Ledger* (1979; Applegarth Follies 1975)

M. Travis Lane

The Thing Outside

A desperate unhappiness lies hereabouts;
like a house pet wants in, wants out, or
courses the back streets, but
nothing diverts its focus long –
neither the moon
whose laden finger stripes the house
nor the attention of a friend
drowning nearby, but swimming hard.

I close my doors.
Its voice comes in the window,
short of breath,
catching its words as if they hurt.
I leave a bit of chopped food on the step.
Almost enough. It grabs and runs.
It's crouching under the bushes there.
It would overwhelm me like a sea
in which I do not choose to swim.
Like Noah on his splinter, I'm afloat.
Like Noah's wife
I tip my glass.
                    'Cheers!' I say
to the dark outside. And the darkness
whispers back.

Night Physics (1994)

Carole Glasser Langille

If I Had My Way

If I had my way I would take you
under the shadow of trees
and tell you things. I would take
one of your hands
in both of mine, below hills
where moss clings
to the curve of rocks. Something in us
is unfailing. As light
as sun through water. Though water
is reckless. Waves crash. From them
the last drop of mist contains
more life than you need to populate a world.
The world is shivering. Listen: Your voice
is a river spilling into an ocean, or night
rushing into a darkening sky. Like coming home late,
the house dark. Who is waiting but someone you once knew
and were not expecting
and were hoping to see again. And there's wine
and cake left from last night.
In the most unexpected places,
you're waiting. Years from now
we won't remember the pact we made: to confess
nothing, not to lean
over the edge of the world.

My children are asleep and friends
have gone home. It is all
enormous. I'm forced
to start small.
If I had my way ...

But each life requires love
it cannot use.
Yes, it is me.
It's the invisible me who won't forget
and who you hold without touching.

In Cannon Cave (1997)

Ross Leckie

First Visit to the Library

Shy, with hands stashed in pockets,
he regards the rows of shiny spines.
The armored light is prehistoric –
the enveloping hush of a 'Please be quiet.'
This is the old fire hall at Pine Point;

the sun twirls down slippery shafts,
dusts itself in a lemon-slice lattice.
Knowledge, he knows, lies in the encyclopedias
in banks in the center of the room,
like puffins on the cliffs of the bird islands.

Along the walls – his heart stops, and starts again –
are the mysteries. He picks *The Discovery
of the Skeleton Key*. He pauses in the shadows:
Little Women by Louisa May Alcott,
which makes him think of little peaches.

Books do and do not contain his loves.
He clambers onto a step ladder reaching
for Tom Swift. She says, 'Careful,'
from behind the large desk. She wears
a tartan skirt with a large safety pin.

The first time he understands his own name is
writing it on library slips, papers scattering
like bread crumbs in the backyard. The weight
of the books under his arm is comfortable.
Life, he suspects, will stretch out in a long line.

The Authority of Roses (1997)

93

Dennis Lee

pen-/ ultimate lady

Pen-
ultimate lady, alive-sweet

skin and sesame:
why do we ever rub con-

tours, if not to conjure
shapes of what we aren't and

crave to be? …
Touching you I am

meat & pronto, I lounge in the chutzpah of
flesh; then woozy with

laughter and midnight and
caring, pure

carnal
panache-you, you, you in your frabjous parade –

how should I
reach for more?

Yet always behind you (this is
why I shy away), barely be-

yond you
is

nothing at all …
Lady,

do not be offended when I
go there.

from *Riffs* (1993)

John B. Lee

The boy is five

The boy is five, running for the farmhouse with a duck on his head. The duck is flapping his wings, beating the boy's ears, hauling at his scalp like a storm shingle hiking its nails. The boy is running, the duck on his head gyrating like a tin roof half torn off, the bill drinking blood. The boy is running, his mad hands flashing like a feather plucker in the belly down, the duck cleated so the toe webs are stretched open and rubbery, adhering to the flesh below the hair. The boy is running for the farmhouse where his grandfather is at the gate jacking the manure from his boots, first one, then the other, so the sheep dung is there on the jack blade whickered with straw, and dark green, lincoln green, cud green, appleshit green, a high sweet rose-garden stink instant and to be relished. The grandfather says nothing. With his eyes says, 'Don't hurt that duck, boy.' Says, 'Ducks are money.' With his eyes. Turns. Walks towards the house. Leaves the boy with the duck on his head like a living hat.

from *Variations on Herb* (1993)

Tim Lilburn

Inanna, Mother, Before The First Days,
When Her Physics Was Young

Sixteen, just, who'll plough my vulva?   I want a farmer.
Daddy's a god, pulls strings with a claw on his hairy harp
    for the shepherd.   He sings, the god, for Dumuzi.
But I want a farmer.
I know him, hey, lambman ... cloverbreathed, milkhand ...
    honey lap ... Dumuzi, him ... bleat-boy, his thigh of flutes. Got it?
                                    I know him.
I want a farmer.   I'm me, insurable legs
    rooted in my brain. I take what I want.

I see you looking at me. Enough to raise the dead, right?
                        as the bishop said to the chorus girl.
I wish. I can't figure it.
I add me up, add me up, add me up, my mirror counts me religiously: hair,
    breath, socket, blood, hair; my breasts swell, whoa-a-a,
                out of control, arguments in a hillbilly metaphysics.
But I'm not pretty.
My geek, boring skin explodes
    in grape bunch, corn ear
    ... papaya, fattening, brown.
They say I've a religious rash.
I say we're born originals, we mustn't end up copies.

Hey, you've got problems? Tell me about it. I've got the big one. Much-o.
                        Look at this.
Look.   Look with terror on the king's colicky 'permanent' erection.
That. So who do you think's got to keep it up there
by bluff of her will's wingspread or the fields faint slack?
You know it, Nick.
And then what'll keep off pogey my flabby temple priesthood,
                    the last romantics,
jaw-banging over sacred wheat, clued in only to yap the sex they've lost
                        between their ears.

I'll tell you.
I've had it,
Earth eats the woman.   I've a blood-ache.
Earth's my blood ache.

Give me a farmer then.
I want a farmer.
My floodplain stomach shivers wheat.
I am lung forests.
I adore everything in pants.
My brains of light want to swing in the trees.
To be fruit, rind, spoiling to flesh, muscle, sweetening
until they choke for breath on a strangled limb.   I become what I see.
I want a farmer.
Floods' afterbirth yolks the humus pubic
moist for him, moist for the farmer.
I'm queen, so what I say goes.   Give me a farmer.
I've more personality than brains.

My mirror has the hots for me. It counts, it counts. I love it.
                              I'm just sixteen,
adored, gleam-tip of the people's milkstare, their white-eyed heart,
                                        their   teeth flashing chests.

I love my vulva too. Ribboned, worship-scented,
                              it is a boat and carries the people.
Stacked vulva, heaven's boat, it staggers
under civic corn from Eridu to Uruk,
Uruk Eridu, the peoples' canoe, reeling, sweet-hilled with corn.
And then my snazzy priesthood, at ten waterside temples, strokes
                    four times its golden guitar, me passing,
them singing, real nice, 'Her breasts are a tree of birds.'

from *From the Great Above She Opened Her Ear to the Great Below* (1988)

Jésus López-Pacheco

Norman Bethune

The most humane Canadian of our age
went to Spain when Spain was crying to the world
'Come and see the spilled blood!'.
'My eyes are overflowing,' he said, *'and clouded with blood.'*
He could not look
at the bloodshed he was seeing.
But the blood of the dead was already
just dead blood.

The most humane Canadian of our age
wrote thirty verses like thirty blasphemies
on the blood spilled by the dead.
Like anti-aircraft, anti-heaven guns
that perhaps were able to shoot down several planes
or even an entire squadron of winged hypocrisies.

The most humane Canadian of our age,
without forgetting the bloodshed,
thought of the living blood still fighting.
And being himself a poet of another kind,
when he saw wounds like *'terrible flowers of flesh',*
he rhymed their edges with stitches
so that the spilling of blood would stop.
But sometimes these flowers suddenly
withered, for they had lost too much blood.
And the blood of the dead was already
just dead blood.

The most humane Canadian of our age
saw how the guns passed from the hands
of the dead and wounded to the living
who had no guns in their hands.

He thought of the blood, of all the blood of the people of Spain,
and saw that it was a sea, a gigantic network of rivers
flowing into other rivers which were flowing into the sea,
into the immense red sea that was defending
life.

The most humane Canadian of our age
climbed on a little truck and went to all the front lines
with bottles of blood. Having discovered
that human veins could flow into human veins,
he founded the 'Servicio Canadiense de Transfusión de Sangre',
'Canadian Blood Transfusion Service'.

Poetic Asylum (1991)

Brent MacKay

Noche

Mescal moon,
pearl button,
saddest light
I've ever seen
on fedora mountain:
                    Sierra Madre.

3 dead cows
by the highway.

A bright blanket
on a breeze.

Tequila:
the mind's limbo
beneath fanpalm.

The King of Bean (1981)

Kim Maltman

The Technology of Metal, Turning

The snow comes down,
blows or drifts,
inanimate, without intention.
Nonetheless, there are parts of the city
where those without shelter
freeze, or huddle over gratings, or
death comes by degree, beginning with this night.
To some it is a comfort to believe
some larger reason moves behind this.
That pleasure is not created, but bestowed.
Heavy snow has come, too,
to the mountains,
and many hunting there are stranded.
It is possible at times like this,
in need of warmth,
to kill and gut a deer,
to see the body, cut, steam violently,
and spend the night inside the freshly opened carcass.
Afterwards this comes to be recounted with such
powerful nostalgia that,
in having been told the story only once,
and with the din of machinery, as well,
around me, so that I had to strain,
and listen with great concentration,
the smell of metal, freshly lathed,
is tinged still with the smell of blood.
It says the soul does not exist,
that there is nothing to diminish pain,
or pleasure,
or to give it permanence.

Technologies/Installations (1990)

Don McKay

The Eye meets Tom Thomson's 'A Rapid'

The eye observes the little rapid furl
into the foreground and the yellow
leaves beside it sing right out –
                                        and moves

up river, in, above
the rapid entering
blackness
here at the heart of the canvas.

A backdrop?   Yes the eye
sees how the dark sets up
the warbling rapid and the leaves'
five-hundred-watt good-bye.
But also how everything's
imperilled, how Alfred Hitchcock
appears in his own show as a waiter
waiting –
              and moves another step to feel
how textured (are you sure
we're doing the right thing how
depthed it draws us to the pool the pool which
brimsmooth for a stone or for the clean
cleaving a canoe can be the perfect
penis entering an angel, make the shapes appear
in darkness, delicate, dramatic
tangle of twigs or opulent autumn clamouring
paint me paint me as the eye
begins to know each crook and gesture of the long and
infinitely innovative
whorehouse
the velvet
closing as a lid behind.

O scenery's not scenery no more/ the stage
has shifted under us, the show
goes on
and on, beyond all ends
the eye imagines, crazy Wagner,
having killed the gods
again, refusing to finish the banquet, lets
have another sunset pal he turns
to eat the audience –
                    that's you
that's the eye, we'd better
wake up and get out of here friend,
if we can.

from *Lependu* (1978)

A.F. Moritz

The Parents

If we ever in our fever woke up
they were with us, catching the sweat in deep cotton
and the delirium, our obscenities,
in softer and still more muffling ears.
We were always in their arms, never more strictly
than when the brain in sickness fell,
spinning in itself, with nothing to stop it.

They stopped it. They always soothed us, making life
possible. And our own bodies worked with them,
hearts kept on beating when we wanted to die:
it was bitter then, but later we were glad,
a muscle knew better than mind that mind would change.

They were part of the earth:
a thing dry, moist, lush, vacant, open,
impenetrable. Love, you went out walking in the wheat laid low
on a moist August evening,
in the field beyond the line of towering hornbeams:
though we didn't know the future, how the tumor
would grow in you, you went out laughing,
you cut your ankles on the blackberry vines.

Didn't I kiss the earth when my wife was safe again
and beside me? Didn't I throw myself
on its thin breast, grind my lips on
its jagged little boulders of baked clay,
when I saw her stretched out, just one more furrow?

We were always given our portions and told, Give thanks.
Does a dog give thanks for food and beatings?
It can remember only a little. To its simplicity
they are always wonderful, it always comes back again
to the place where they befell it, cringing and eager.

Song of Fear (1992)

Jane Southwell Munro

Wood Box

If time is a local muscle
bound to the bone it moves....
If time bears itself, as a zygote does a baby....
If time curls round us like the jet stream, circulating
atoms of oxygen in and out of bodies....

I wouldn't ask
except I dreamt of fire – dreamt twice
not on the flat screen of my darkened mind,
I dreamt of fire in virtual reality – dreamt
then woke, and still the dream went on.

Fire drifted,
fingered things, claimed this and that.
Ran along beams, scrambled up logs.
Then, convinced, drove a root through the floor.
Burst, amaryllis, above the roof.

Smoke like a wool rug about my shoulders.
Choked, sitting upright, eyes open –
staring at floating petals of flame –
Father! the cry I tried to make.

When the dream left me in my own home,
in a body I could move,
room to room, I checked on sleeping children.

Five months earlier
the first blaze sprinted across the drapes.
I stumbled to the window, shook the pleats,
then waking further, saw
only moonlight spattered on the walls.

Did I know? Foresee
the fire in my parents' home? My mother's death?

The oldest brain projects a web
then sways in the middle of her trap.
Out-foxing logic, our dream-maker
winds a silver screen limb to limb
and catches the fog of a dripping forest.

Surely the house fire was not time's arson....
And my mother's action –
her plunge into the burning house to grab a hose –
sprang true: her free, predictable, response....

Ashes. Ashes in my hand.
Fire terrifies me –
for myself, for my family.
Maybe love is coal or oil or gas
and I am wood,
laid between others, in a wooden box.

Grief Notes and Animal Dreams (1995)

Michael Ondaatje / Lola Lemire Tostevin, trans.

From *Elimination Dance/La danse éliminatoire*

Those who are allergic to the sea

Ceux qui sont allergiques à la mer

Those who have written to the age-old brotherhood of Rosicrucians
for a free copy of their book 'The Mastery of Life' in order to release
the inner consciousness and to experience (in the privacy of the home)
momentary flights of the soul

Ceux qui ont écrit à la société des Rose-Croix pour une copie gratuite
du livre *La Maîtrise de la Vie* afin de libérer leur conscient intérieur et
d'éprouver dans l'intimité du foyer, les vols passagers de l'âme

Anyone who has been penetrated by a mountie

Toute personne qui s'est fait pénétrer par un membre de la
Gendarmerie royale du Canada

Men who have never touched a whippet

Les hommes qui n'ont jamais touché un whippet

Women who gave up the accordion because of pinched breasts

Les femmes qui ont abandonné l'accordéon à cause de seins pincés

Any lover who has gone into a flower shop on Valentine's Day and
asked for clitoris when he meant clematis

Tout amant qui, à la Saint-Valentin, est entré dans une boutique de fleuriste et a demandé pour un clitoris au lieu d'une clématite

Anyone with pain

Toute personne qui souffre

(1991)

P.K. Page

Planet Earth

It has to be spread out, the skin of this planet,
has to be ironed, the sea in its whiteness;
and the hands keep on moving,
smoothing the holy surfaces.

In Praise of Ironing   *Pablo Neruda*

It has to be loved the way a laundress loves her linens,
the way she moves her hands caressing the fine muslins
knowing their warp and woof,
like a lover coaxing, or a mother praising.
It has to be loved as if it were embroidered
with flowers and birds and two joined hearts upon it.
It has to be stretched and stroked.
It has to be celebrated.
O this great beloved world and all the creatures in it.
It has to be spread out, the skin of this planet.

The trees must be washed, and the grasses and mosses.
They have to be polished as if made of green brass.
The rivers and little streams with their hidden cresses
and pale-coloured pebbles
and their fool's gold
must be washed and starched or shined into brightness,
the sheets of lake water
smoothed with the hand
and the foam of the oceans pressed into neatness.
It has to be ironed, the sea in its whiteness

and pleated and goffered, the flower-blue sea
the protean, wine-dark, grey, green, sea
with its metres of satin and bolts of brocade.
And sky – such an O! overhead – night and day
must be burnished and rubbed
by hands that are loving
so the blue blazons forth
and the stars keep on shining
within and above
and the hands keep on moving.

It has to be made bright, the skin of this planet
till it shines in the sun like gold leaf.
Archangels then will attend to its metals
and polish the rods of its rain.
Seraphim will stop singing hosannas
to shower it with blessings and blisses and praises
and, newly in love,
we must draw it and paint it
our pencils and brushes and loving caresses
smoothing the holy surfaces.

Hologram (1997)

The glosa: 'the opening quatrain written by another poet; followed by four
ten-line stanzas, their concluding lines taken consecutively from the quatrain;
their sixth and ninth lines rhyming with the borrowed tenth. Used by the poets
of the Spanish court, the form dates back to the late 14th and early 15th century.'

Kenneth Radu

The Road Taken

The graveyard road is clear of snow.
A perfect picture of a cold drive
between arches of trees, it leads unbroken
to juncos and jays among the brown wreaths.
The air is white and blue as the breath
of a ghost and the city is a sound
elsewhere. Here your unbroken voice
is loud with the weight of meditation
upon last things, upon the fine job
done by diggers who keep the road clear,
so there's never any stalling on your way
to deep thoughts and dead flowers.

Letter to a Distant Father (1987)

Roberta Rees

One of the popular boys

One of the popular boys picks me up in a purple car, don't know why
me except maybe his girlfriend told him to fuck off, just fuck right off,
probably for drinking. Picks me up in a purple Pontiac smells like Irish
Spring and hockey pads and rye whisky. Hands me a brown chicken
clucking, Could you hold Louise, she wants to come to this party, can't
leave Louise home, somebody might eat her, hey Louise, hey chick-
chick-chick. Holding Louise, heartbeat my thigh, buck-buck-buck her
throat my fingers, feathers my crotch, warm oh warm. He shoves the
car into Drive, floors it. Through Bellevue, the Frank Slide, Blairmore,
Coleman, up the Forestry Trunk Road, the hair black curled on his
neck warm skin soap booze air freshener and Louise, Louise. And i
can't think of a thing to say, don't know what i'm doing here holding
his chicken except his fingers hard and brown from working the mine,
me one year away in the city back for summer and my crotch, my
crotch. Fish-tailing up the Forestry Road and the pines,
mmmmmmmmm the pines, not talking touching nothing. I carry
Louise into the cabin on my arm, pulse and warm skin and feathers,
put her up on a rafter, Be safe, Louise, be safe. He talks with his
friends, laughs and talks and turns his face so he can look sideways at
his girlfriend talking and laughing with her friends, drinks and drinks.
I stand by the door invisible, cool air mountains black jagged pines the
pulse in my groin Louise up in the rafter throat song. He holds his
glass up to Louise, his friends hold their glasses up, beer whisky gin,
she dip dip dips. All the cheekbones, eyes blue green brown lavender
indigo chartreuse dun chestnut hazel, fingers scooped tapered pillowed
flat thick bony spread hooked fisted, rye on their breath gin on their
breath, beer baby duck cherry liqueur, voices in their throats, and i
want to go home with them all of them talk to their mothers and
fathers, tell me what your bodies remember how you sleep what you
eat how you breathe in Keilbossa cottage cheese gnocchi vereniki
halubsha gripe water toilet water tobacco and the smells of your
sleeping what you see when you close your eyes. Her lids drop and she
sways on the rafter forward back forward, groans, falls. Scrabbles in
circles on the floor, clucks and moans and white mucous drips from

her beak. They stand around her laughing, Look at the goddamn chicken she's goddamn drunk. When I pick her up, Hey, Leave her there, she's havin' a good time, hold her shaking to my chest, You're okay you'll be okay Louise Louise chick-chick-chick. Drops me off the sun coming up over the mountains, the purple Pontiac vibrates in front of our house, Louise passed out on my knee, See ya. Hardly looks at me, purple Pontiac in the sun, humming in the sun, away. Or in a white Buick, parked on the old Frank Road, limestone boulders black against the sky, Turtle Mountain black against the sky and Frank Lake breathing cold, so pissed his eyes flutter, lays his head on my chest, You're too good for me she won't even talk to said she still loves me what are you doing with, Jesus Jesus Jesus. And in Calgary in the dark on the floor his hand stroking my face his voice in the dark on my cheek, She'll come back I know she will just has to try it out he's a med. student she needs that I can wait two more years before I graduate I can wait. Smells like limes. Pulse in my groin ache in my groin his hand on my forehead cheek eyelids temple that's all. Twenty-one a drug dealer out of prison let me show you baby had to think love not desire not lust not i want to pull you inside flex my muscles young and wet and strong.

from *Eyes Like Pigeons* (1992)

John Reibetanz

Verdigris

Pulled
from a shipwreck near Marathon
a boy once bronze.

Not revived
because he never was alive,
this Greek boy's bronze

the real, dead thing,
no figure for
skin in love with sun.

The blind sea took him in,
plied him with its dark
wine, corrupted him

into its image: verdigris, pure
green of the deaf blue deep, not a whisper
of the sun's brazen gong.

* * *

Verdigris, rust of brass or bronze,
betrayed the scientific eye
of Bacon, distracted from the cold
prose of this 'putrefaction'
by its 'orient and fine colour.'

Verdigris – the very word corrupted:
'vert de Grece,' green of Greece,
the terminal syllable rusting
into misty 'gris,'
the grey-green of a Norman dawn.

* * *

Greek boy, your green figure
rises from the sea
like a dark sun, like life itself,

to mime the life of words
which, never living, green
through their corruption:

orphaned, shipped and wronged
on the wind, lost and recovered,
your green silence figures our green sounds.

Your foster-mother knows: Athena,
immortal giver of the long-lived olive tree –
green, tenacious, bitter.

Midland Swimmer (1996)

William Robertson

The Man Who Lost a Foot

A snowy Remembrance Day spent
remembering men I never knew
and getting my children to stay quiet
through the Last Post, the minute
of silence, and the bilingual prayers
live from Ottawa broadcast
like a sports event
with lots of 'Over to you, Ernie' and
'Thanks, Dick, here's a man who lost
a foot in a propeller, and he was
lucky'
My children are appalled
by such luck

                    my finely clothed daughter
who is black, tall, and lovely
and weekly is told how lucky she is
to be so slim and tall
every year reports the word
nigger has a use this far north

my wife's first child
so white, blonde, and blue-eyed
you'd think in any country
so close to surfers' beaches
he'd be out of reach
of slurs attached to his last name:
'What's a nazi?' he asks
'They called me a nazi'
and when I explain his lineage
he tells me I'm lucky
so I tell him my first day
at school in an outpost
of the British Empire

cornered by the backstop
once they'd heard where I was born
three cunning classmates slanting
their eyes and saying 'You
don't look Chinese' and me
wanting to hurt them all
telling them instead about Japan
my missionary parents
and one brought his face up close
spat 'I lost an uncle
to them Japanese'
and I retorted 'I lost two uncles'
and my son asks 'Did you lose them
                    to the nazis?'

Adult Language Warning (1991)

Robyn Sarah

Stormblue

'You're rich, and you want to be loved like a poor man.'
— *Les enfants du paradis*

The way a woman loves a man
without money: for the holes
in his socks, for the tilt
of his eyebrows, for his voice
singing a song or murmuring
behind a door, for the fragrant
smoke of his pipe bluing the air
in the small old cozy cluttered room,
for his patched elbows, his
tweedy jackets from the Nearly New,
for the blind intelligence
of his body in love, for his hands,
quiet on the table, their dance
in the air when he speaks,
for the mole
on the back of his neck, for a few
old jokes that he likes to tell,
for his laugh,
for the way his hair sticks up
in the morning, for the cleft
in his chin, for a dimple
(seldom seen) in his left cheek,
for his dreams, and the light
that they put in his eyes
evenings of dreamy talk —

For the blue of his eyes
that she calls
his baby eyes
that grow stormblue
in anger at being loved
for the foolish things
she loves him for,
because they are all he has
to give her,
because he knows
that she knows
he will never
have more.

Questions About The Stars (1998)

Barbara Schott

Driving Mostly Prairie

I want your bathtub where you can find
me. Like the night before last. Haven't

seen an antelope in years. It was a dry
spring. A day like any other. But how

do we read the simile. The sloped leaves
of the wild sorrel. I can't cope with

the logic of those rock piles you keep
pointing out. I realize your father was a man

of science. If I wasn't so particular it
wouldn't matter. What I want is

a river of my own.

Leach the sky of stars, the night-teal drain.
The moon is a plug. It's you who tells me

you're over your head. The dripping
outside the window is no illusion.

Icicles fall from the eaves and decay,
the jade plant drops a leaf. Pure thought

is not possible. It seems you can come
to harm just closing your eyes. There are bits

of myself in the tub, if you care
to look.

If I hadn't spent myself
on my otherness. If I had the strategies

of a single river. In time I will learn to forget
myself, step out, indifferent as rain.

You mustn't compare me
to the landscape. I wasn't with you.

Grass is inconsolable. In Saskatchewan
the sun travels along

railroad tracks. The whip-poor-will sleeps
by day. But the stars shine for anyone.

Memoirs of an Almost Expedition (1999)

Carolyn Smart

October

Those fallen leaves, pale supplicants,
have much to teach us of surrender,
how, wrapped in autumn's incense
they unfurl their flags to the wind

Every year I want to kneel in damp soil
and say farewell to blessed things:
the swift geese as they shout each to each
above the treetops, the white nicotinia
at my door, still releasing its fragrance
against the chill of evening,
the memory of a much-loved hand
the last day I held it

There was early morning light rich as silk,
the flash of late fireflies
amidst the cedar,
cows' tails whisking in the amber fields,
the chiaroscuro of a moth's wing

Goodbye, brief lives,
ablaze with tenderness;
today the glory of the leaves
is enough, for I am learning anew
to release all I cannot hold,
these moments of luminous grace
saying Here and here is beauty,
here grief: this is the way to come home

The Way To Come Home (1992)

Douglas Burnet Smith

The Mask of Clear Air

Who is the one unzipping
your future
to reveal nothing
but rotten flesh

Who is the one in the glittering darkness
of his own salt-filled eyes
wearing the mask
of clear air

> Who is the one that shouts
> *You! Hair! Scab! Race!*
> *You! Bright shield!*
> *It is the blood of fossils*
> *that stains your blunt glowing nails*

Who is the one
printing the names of trees
on your lashes
the one tearing hooves
from between your teeth

Ladder to the Moon (1988)

Francis Sparshott

Stations of Loss

1

Growing older is this –
nothing really,
folks do it every day
who can't do anything else at all hardly.
It is only not to be young again
that's hard, that's hard.

2

Where did I leave
youth and the gift
of rhyming? I put them down,
can't lay my hands on them.
Not that I use them for anything
lately, but I get restless
without them, can't settle down
for wondering where they are.

3

Wordsworth has written his last poem.
Gritting his teeth, he writes
another poem.

4

The asphodel meadows where the dead walk
give scant grazing.   Schmoos
browse in the wompom and
nobody knows what silphium
was but it must have been
great.

5

Death comes for Jesus who is coming
for death.   It has the effect of slick wit
but goes on too long.   The unheard tree
sibilant in a forest
of trees.   X marks the immaculate
spot.

6

The first he had made
the last he would make
behold it was good
and he was alone and
no god saw
he made his one world and
he blew it.

7

In the last year of Victoria's century
grandmother, shawled and cosy by the fire,
falls into a dream of Franklin's men
in winter, crawling from the cracked hull,
hauling Sir John's rosewood writing desk
over the boulders of a black shoreline
into a cold, unsettled continent.

The Cave of Trophonius and Other Poems (1983)

Colleen Thibadeau

The Glass Cupboard

Lights from the Highway sparser, softer now
and the Gorst lights gone and their house gone
away, just lost rib to new life in dark seas,
just dark seven sleepers gone seasabout the foot of our hill,
just the foot of the hill and a great cave opening up.

Lights from the glass cupboard !spark! the house dark;
And it's up to the glass cupboard now! It looms
at James' headheight, three paces from kitchen sink,
one from table, length approximately my armspan, crafted
by an Albertan who loved the bush, the hills.

The Bay Highway kindles to blue Italian grotto glasses;
and green glasses, safe-and-wide as Sweden; and cheap
little ruby liqueurs sing; and cocktail Libbys supermart
violent and fresh from fists that swung axes, pounded down a territory
and rolled Malcolm Lowry into the soundmad surf dazzling no warning ...

By an Albertan who loved the bush, the hills,
who made this cupboard ark that tends the tides
of dream. *They light, they guard* the house,
glow like an icon of Mike Todd, thirty-odd glasses,
touched off by random headlights moving toward the Bay.

The Artemesia Book: Poems Selected and New (1991)

Derk Wynand

Ferry

Ours was the last of the cars to squeeze onto the ferry,
all our prayers directed to the controllers of traffic
finally answered. Yes, we were blessed.

On the car radio that long day, those who delighted
in promoting our guilt had spoken of God become flesh,
more precisely, of a deity in diapers, an image
that seemed to touch on the reasons for our travel:
family, the habitual Christmas. Deity in diapers —
wow! This theology we thought we could live with!

Granny had laid her corsage with its braids of tinsel
and arabesques of green spray-paint on the back seat
beside her and complained she was tired. No wonder,
all of us talking nonstop and everyone on the radio
talking nonstop and mostly nonsense at that.

A few days before, she complained, at the shrink's,
she had failed all the tests that had had her spell
words backwards, retrace geometric shapes backwards,
count backwards from 100 by sevens or eights.
Every one of the clocks she'd been asked to draw
came out totally wrong, their numbers all bunched
together in a low corner or off to one side.

We tried to console her, trying at the same time
to hide our own anxieties over how long it took us
to spell 'world,' for example, backwards, to count
past 93, 86, 79.... We said, how can doing anything
backwards be a sign of either failure or success?

Unconvinced, she refused later to join in our game
of naming the relatives waiting for us across the strait,
game that our kids quickly won. She kept looking at them,
at us, then down at the grey water as the ferry slowly
took us across, the muscles of her face twitching,
as if there were something important she had to remember

Closer to Home (1997)

Jan Zwicky

Open Strings

E, laser of the ear, ear's
vinegar, bagpipes
in a tux, the sky's blue, pointed;

A, youngest of the four, cocksure
and vulnerable, the white kid
on the basketball team – immature,
ambitious, charming,
indispensable; apprenticed
to desire;

D is the tailor
who sewed the note 'I shall always love you'
into the hem of the village belle's wedding dress,
a note not discovered until ten years later in New York
where, poor and abandoned, she was ripping up the skirt
for curtains, and he came,
and he married her;

G, cathedral of the breastbone,
Oak-light, earth;

it's air they offer us,
but not the cool draught of their half-brothers
the harmonics, no,
a bigger wind, the body
snapped out like a towel, air
like the sky above the foothills,
like the desire to drown,

a place of worship,
a laying down of arms.
                        Open strings
are ambassadors from the republic of silence.
They are the name of that moment when you realize
clearly, for the first time,
you will die. After illness,
the first startled breath.

Songs for Relinquishing the Earth (1998)

Biographical Notes

Bert Almon was born in Texas in 1943. He teaches creative writing at the University of Alberta. *Earth Prime* was the seventh of his eight collections of poetry.

Mia Anderson lives on a farm near Mount Forest, Ontario, when not studying in Toronto. Is just completing an M.Div., leading to ordination as an anglican priest (D.V.) in Huron diocese. Was an actor for 25-odd years before poetry claimed her, with *Appetite* (Brick) in 1988, *ChâteauPuits '81* (Oolichan) in 1992, *Practising Death* (St. Thomas Poetry Series) 1997, and the fourth (not yet finished) *The Shambles*, an excerpt of which won the National Magazine Award in 1992.

Les Arnold taught English at the University of Western Ontario for several years before returning to a teaching career in England, his country of origin. Before his untimely death he had published a children's book and five books of poetry. *Les Arnold: Uncollected Writings and Tributes* (Jeremy Hooker, ed.) was published in England, 1995.*

Mike Barnes has published poetry and prose in numerous magazines and anthologies. *Calm Jazz Sea* (Brick Books, 1996) was shortlisted for the Gerald Lampert Memorial Award. His stories have appeared in *The Journey Prize Anthology* and in *Best Canadian Stories. Aquarium,* a collection of short stories, was published by The Porcupine's Quill in 1999 and awarded first prize in the Danuta Gleed Literary Competition.

Rhonda Batchelor was born in Brantford Ontario but has lived in Victoria B.C. since 1973. Her published books include *Bearings* (Brick Books), *Interpreting Silence* (Beach Holme Publishers) and *Weather Report* (also Beach Holme). She is a bookstore manager and publisher of the Reference West series of chapbooks which she co-founded with her late husband Charles Lillard.

---

* Not prepared by the author.

Julie Berry, ex-tobacco harvester, ex-psychiatric nurse's aid, and ex-market gardener, teaches kindergarten in her native St. Thomas, Ontario, where she lives with her four sons. She has been involved in the peace movement for years. Her poetry has appeared in such journals as *Room of One's Own, Quarry,* and *Canadian Forum. worn thresholds* is her first book.

Guy Birchard is too good a writer and too smart a guy not to be shining up the hours wherever he is, but we've lost track of him. Here's something sharp he said once: 'what this country needs is more good unpublished poets.'*

Walid Bitar was born in Beirut, Lebanon in 1961. His collections of poetry are *Maps With Moving Parts* (Brick Books) and *2 Guys on Holy Land* (Wesleyan University Press).

Marianne Bluger has published six poetry collections, three of which were with Brick. *Gusts* (Penumbra, 1998) was the first book of English tanka to be published in Canada. Her next collection is *Scissors, Paper, Woman* an autobiographical, feminist work using the imagist and lyric forms she began to experiment with in the seventies when she was married to a Zen master.

Robert Bringhurst was born in 1946. He lives, most of the time, as far north or west or south or east as he can get.

David Bromige, Canadian author, English-born, sexagenarian, often found in ex-hometown, Vancouver, resides in California. Thirty-two titles published – poetry, short stories, a novella, a novel. Selected poems, *Desire*, from Black Sparrow, won the Western States award in 1988. Due in 2000: *As in 'T' As In 'Tether'*, poetry from Chax Press in Tucson.

Colin Browne is completing a new film, *Altar*, based on a photograph of the ship's company of H.M.C.S. Mayflower circa 1941. A new book, *Fossil,* is nearing completion as is a collection of essays about the documentary impulse in poetry, photography and cinema.

Julie Bruck's first book, *The Woman Downstairs*, received QSPELL's A.M. Klein Award in 1994. Her recent work won a National Magazine Award for poetry, and has appeared in such magazines as *Carousel, Ceilidh, Ms.,* and *The New Yorker*. A native Montrealer, she has taught writing at Concordia University, and has been a regular contributor to CBC Radio. She lives in San Francisco, California.

Anne Carson was born in Canada and teaches ancient Greek for a living. She spends most of her time otherwise painting volcanoes.

Where the hell did those twenty-five years go? For the past eleven of them, Brian Charlton has taught English at Clarke Road Secondary School in London, enjoying the wit and wisdom of younger writers. By the time the anthology is published, you can refer to me as retired.

Hilary Clark lives in Saskatoon, where she teaches English and Women's Studies at the University of Saskatchewan. *More Light* is her first book of poetry. A second book, *Two Heavens* (Hagios Press, Saskatoon), also appeared in 1998.

Karen Connelly is the author of six books, the most recent being a new collection of poetry called *The Border Surrounds Us*. She is at work on a novel set in Burma.

Méira Cook is a writer living and working in Vancouver. Her first novel, *The Blood Girls*, was recently published.

Marlene Cookshaw was born and raised in Southern Alberta. She studied at the University of Lethbridge before moving to the west coast of B.C. in 1979. She has been a member of *The Malahat Review*'s editorial board since 1985, and is currently Acting Editor. Her poetry, fiction and reviews have been published in such magazines as: *The American Voice, Arc, Books in Canada, Capilano Review, Fiddlehead, Mississippi Review, Prairie Fire, Quarry, Raddle Moon,* and *Waves*. Her work has also been featured on CBC Radio.

Joan Crate lives, teaches, raises kids, and writes in Red Deer, Alberta.

Her second collection of poetry, *Foreign Homes* will be published by Brick Books in 2001.

Michael Crummey has published two books of poetry, *Arguments with Gravity* and *Hard Light*, as well as a collection of stories, *Flesh & Blood*. *Hard Light* was nominated for the 1999 Milton Acorn People's Poetry Award.

Greg Curnoe was born in London in 1936. He studied art at Beal Technical School in London, at Doon School of Fine Arts in Kitchener, and at the Ontario College of Art in Toronto (where he achieved the distinction of failing in his final year) and for the rest of his life as a perpetual autodidact. He was a founder of the Nihilist Spasm Band, the Forest City Gallery, and *Region* magazine.*

Lynn Davies's non-fiction has appeared in many Canadian magazines and her stories for children have been published in various anthologies. After a 16 year sojourn in Nova Scotia, Lynn now lives with her family on McLeod Hill, New Brunswick. *The Bridge That Carries the Road*, her first book, was nominated for the 1999 Governor General's Award for Poetry.

A member of Renga, **Patrick Deane** began a life's collaboration with Sheila McColm after the Renga appeared. He teaches at the University of Western Ontario, where he is Chair of English. He has published two further books, neither of them poetry.

Barry Dempster is the author of six books of poetry, two collections of short stories, a children's book and a novel. He lives in Holland Landing, Ontario, just north of Toronto.

John Donlan is a poetry editor at Brick Books. He works as a reference librarian in British Columbia at the Vancouver Public Library. His books of poetry are *Domestic Economy* (Brick Books, 1990, reprinted 1997), *Baysville* (House of Anansi Press, 1993), and *Green Man* (Ronsdale Press, 1999).

A member of Renga, **Peggy Dragišić** (now using her maiden name,

Roffey) has a fatal attraction to symmetry: she studied English (and taught a little) for 16 years, worked in health care for 16 years, and is now trying to reactivate a life in literature (teaching? criticism? writing?) for at least another 16 years before retirement. She lives in London with her husband, youngest daughter, and Rufus the dog.

Marilyn Dumont, a descendant of Gabriel Dumont, is a writer from Alberta. Following a career in film and video production, she completed a M F A at the University of British Columbia. Subsequently, she taught English and Creative Writing in secondary and post-secondary institutions in Vancouver where she continues to work as the Coordinator of the First Nations Student Centre at Simon Fraser University. Her poems are anthologized in *The Road Home, Writing the Circle, The Colour of Resistance, Looking at the Words of Our People,* and the *Anthology of Canadian Native Literature in English.*

E.F. Dyck is a writer, editor, and critic who practices rhetoric in central Alberta. He is the author of four books of poetry and the editor of three collections of essays. Most recently, he is the author of an on-line work in progress called *The South Ram River Rambles* and the editor of the new on-line literary magazine called *RedNeck.*

Patrick Friesen is a poet, lyricist, scriptwriter and playwright who has published ten books of poetry. His most recent book is *Carrying the Shadow* (Beach Holme, 1999). He teaches creative writing at Kwantlen University College in Vancouver.

Cherie Geauvreau was born in Windsor in 1948. She has excellent writers' credentials, having been a cook, a house cleaner, a forklift operator, and having worked in pharmaceuticals and restaurant management. She also served short stints in various institutions of higher learning and in the convent. She lives on the West Coast where she writes in a small cabin in the woods and works in her community as a fierce advocate for women and children. Her work was featured in the 20th Anniversary *Capilano Review,* as well as *Prism International, The American Voice* and *Prairie Fire,* among others. *Even the Fawn Has Wings* is her first book.

Susan Goyette, originally from St. Bruno, now lives in Cole Harbour, Nova Scotia. Her first book of poems, *The True Names of Birds* published by Brick Books in 1998, was shortlisted for both the Pat Lowther and Gerald Lampert Awards. It was also nominated for the Governor General's award for poetry. She's currently working on her second collection of poetry.

Neile Graham's poetry, fiction, and nonfiction has been published in Canada, the U.S., and the U.K. Her first poetry collection, *Seven Robins* (Penumbra Press), appeared in 1983, her second, *Spells for Clear Vision* from Brick Books, was shortlisted for the 1994 Pat Lowther Award, and her third, *Blood Memory*, will appear from Buschek Books in 2000.

Terry Griggs has published a collection of short stories, *Quickening*, which was short-listed for a Governor General's Award, and a novel, *The Lusty Man*. She is currently working on a new novel, and has completed a novel for children. *Harrier*, a chapbook, was her first publication. She lives on Manitoulin Island.

Don Gutteridge, a native of Point Edward, Ontario, and graduate of the University of Western Ontario, is the author of seven novels and twelve books of poetry. He is a Professor emeritus from the Faculty of Education at Western.

Naomi Guttman teaches literature and creative writing at Hamilton College in Clinton, New York. She is working on two collections of poetry and a book of short stories. *Reasons for Winter* won the 1992 QSPELL award.

Phil Hall's first book, *Eighteen Poems*, was published in Mexico City in 1973. Since then he has published three chapbooks, a cassette of labour songs, and eight other books of poetry, four of those with Brick Books. Among his titles are: *A Minor Operation, Why I Haven't Written, Old Enemy Juice* and *The Unsaid*. His last book, a long poem, *Hearthedral: A Folk-Hermetic*, appeared from Brick in 1996. He works as an editor and a teacher. He lives in Toronto.

J.A. Hamilton is the author of four books shortlisted for various awards. She has won *Prism International, This Magazine, Event* and *Paragraph* contests as well as the League of Canadian Poets' Canadian Poetry Chapbook Contest.

Maureen Harris is an editor and writer living in Toronto, and an occasional lecturer in the Division of the Environment at the University of Toronto. In her earlier life she worked as a librarian within the University of Toronto, and as a bookstore clerk at Writers & Co. She is working on a second volume of poetry provisionally titled *Learning My Place.*

Brian Henderson is the author of seven collections of poetry (including a deck of visual poem-cards). His work has appeared in a number of small magazines over the years and in the seventies he was a founding editor of RUNE. He worked in educational publishing for most of his career but recently has become the director of Wilfrid Laurier University Press. He has two children and lives with the most wonderful woman in the world in Ashburn, Ontario.

Cornelia Hoogland writes and teaches in London, Ontario. Her third book of poetry, *You are Home,* is currently under review. A reading of her young adult play, *Salmonberry: a West Coast Fairy Tale* is premiering in Athens, Greece in 2000. Her first children's novel, *Jordan's Getting Married* is looking for a publisher.

Helen Humphreys is the author of three previous books of poetry published by Brick Books: *Gods and Other Mortals* (1986), *Nuns Looking Anxious, Listening to Radios* (1990), and *The Perils of Geography* (1995). Her novel *Leaving Earth* (HarperCollins, 1997) has been published in nine countries and won the 1998 City of Toronto Book Award. She lives and writes in Kingston, Ontario.

Francis Itani has published eight books, the most recent being *Leaning, Leaning Over Water* (HarperCollins, 1998). She has been awarded the CBC Literary Award three times for her fiction. She lives in Ottawa.

A.R. Kazuk is an Associate Professor teaching Canadian Literature at the University of Lethbridge. He has published widely in the reviews and has three books, *Microphones* (1987), *Millions of Acres* (1985), and *Dizains* (1990). He is working on a new collection called *Walking Into the Mandala*. He lives in Southern Alberta with his wife and two small children and is trying to convince her that they should get a dog.

Janice Kulyk Keefer is the author of nine books of poetry, fiction, and literary criticism, and a contributor to numerous anthologies. She has twice been nominated for a Governor General's Award, and twice won first prize in both the CBC Radio Literary Competition and the National Magazine Awards. *Travelling Ladies* was one of ten works of fiction chosen for *Ms.* magazine's International Fiction List; her newest novel, *The Green Library*, was nominated for a Governor General's Award and was published in Germany. *Marrying the Sea* was nominated for the Pat Lowther award, and won the 1999 Marian Engel Award for a woman writer in mid-career, as well as the 1999 Canadian Authors Association Award for Poetry. She teaches at the University of Guelph and lives in Eden Mills, Ontario.

Michael Kenyon lives on Pender Island. His most recent publications are *Durable Tumblers* (Oolichan Books, stories), and *Winter Wedding* (Reference West, a chapbook of poems).

Don Kerr is a poet, editor, playwright, and teacher living in Saskatoon. His first collection of short stories, *Love and the Bottle*, is being published by Coteau Books.

Lyn King was born in Ireland and immigrated to Canada in 1959. She lives and works in Toronto.

August Kleinzahler, editor of *News and Weather: Seven Canadian Poets*, is himself a significant poet, best known in the U.S. *Storm Over Hackensack* won the 1985 Bay Area Book Reviewers' Award; *Earthquake Weather* was nominated for a National Book Critics Circle Award for Poetry in 1989. *Like Cities, Like Storms*, a new and selected, was published in Australia in 1992. His most recent collection is *Red Sauce, Whiskey and Snow*, 1995.*

Robert Kroetsch is a poet, novelist and essayist. He is retired from the University of Manitoba and currently lives in Winnipeg.

The Poetry of M. Travis Lane first appeared in *Five Poets* (Cornell, 1960). Since then she has brought out *An Inch or So of Garden, Poems 1968–1972, Homecomings, Divinations and Shorter Poems* (Pat Lowther Prize, 1980), *Walking Under the Nebulae, Reckonings,* and *Solid Things.* A ninth book, *Temporary Shelter,* appeared from Goose Lane Editions in 1993.

Carole Glasser Langille, originally from New York, now lives in Lunenburg, Nova Scotia. She is the author of another book of poetry, *All That Glitters in Water,* and the children's book, *Where the Wind Sleeps,* a Canadian Children's Book Centre Choice for 1996–1997. Her second book of poetry *In Cannon Cave* was shortlisted for a Governor General's Award in 1997.

Ross Leckie was born in Lachine, Quebec and studied English and Philosophy at McGill and Education at the University of Alberta, before taking a Creative Writing Masters at Concordia and a Ph.D. in English at the University of Toronto. His poems have appeared in such journals as *The Antigonish Review, Ariel, Descant, The Fiddlehead, Denver Quarterly, The New Republic, Southwest Review,* and *American Literary Review.* His first collection of poetry, *A Slow Light,* was published by Véhicule Press. He lives in Prince George, British Columbia and teaches English Literature and Creative Writing at the University of Northern British Columbia.

Dennis Lee was born in Toronto in 1939. He has written *Civil Elegies, The Gods,* and a number of collections of children's poetry.

Internationally acclaimed, award-winning author of 30 books, John B. Lee is the only two-time winner of the People's Poetry Award (1993, 1995) and the winner in 1995 of the prestigious $10,000 Tilden Award for poetry (CBC Radio/ *Saturday Night* magazine). His most recent book, *Stella's Journey* (Black Moss Press, 1999) completes *The Highgate Trilogy.* Mr Lee lives in Brantford, Ontario with is wife Cathy and their sons, Dylan and Sean-Paul.

Tim Lilburn is the author of five books of poems and a collection of essays, *Living in the World as if It Were Home* (1999). His most recent book of poetry, *To the River*, won the Saskatchewan Book of the Year Award, while his essays received the Saskatchewan Nonfiction Award.

Jésus López-Pacheco's work as a poet, novelist and playwright has been acclaimed by readers and critics in Spain and the Hispanic world. *Poetic Asylum* was his first collection of poems to be published in English, but his work has been translated into most European languages. His last book, *Ecologas y Urbanas* was published in 1996. Jésus López-Pacheco died on April 6, 1997.*

Brent MacKay lives in Vancouver after a long hiatus in Spain. He writes, but mostly he conjures up schemes to go south.

Kim Maltman was born near Medicine Hat, grew up nearby, and is a member (together with Roo Borson and Andy Patton) of the collaborative writing group Pain Not Bread, whose first book *Introduction to the Introduction to Wang Wei* will be published by Brick Books in Spring 2000.

A member of Renga, Sheila McColm teaches English and Women's Studies at the University of Western Ontario, and reads novels and histories more than poems now. But there are other forms of magic: she married Patrick, had a daughter, Petra, and a son, Colin, and in free time rides her horse, Alchemy.

Don McKay has been editing, etc., for Brick Books since way back when, when things were pretty hands-on (Stan's hands, mostly). *Lependu* was an attempt to invoke the trickster in London, Ontario, and wound up without the author's name on the title page. Was that our master stroke (that is, yet another of them) or evidence that the book had succeeded in its aim?

A.F. Moritz has published three books with Brick, *Song of Fear* (1992), *Mahoning*, (1994), and *Rest on the Flight into Egypt* (1999). He has also written *A Houseboat on the Styx* (1998), a long poem, and two translations in collaboration with his wife, Theresa Moritz, from the work of Ludwig Zeller: *Body of Insomnia* (1996), poems, and *Rio Loa: Station of Dreams* (1999), a novel. Moritz's poetry has received honours including the Award in Literature of the American Academy and Institute of Arts and Letters, a Guggenheim Foundation fellowship, an Ingram Merrill Foundation fellowship, and selection to the Princeton Series of Contemporary Poets. Other collections of his poems are *Here* (1975), *Black Orchid* (1981), *The Visitation* (1983), *The Tradition* (1986), *The Ruined Cottage* (1993), and *Phantoms in the Ark* (1994). He has lived since 1974 in Toronto, where he works as a writer and as a lecturer at the University of Toronto.

Jane Southwell Munro grew up and raised a family in Vancouver. The author of two previous collections of poetry, *Daughters,* and *The Trees Just Moved Into A Season of Other Shapes,* she has travelled widely in Europe and Asia, holds a doctorate in Adult Education, and has taught Creative Writing at UBC and Kwantlen University College. She lives with her husband in a house in the woods on the west coast of Vancouver Island.

It's a little-known fact that *Elimination Dance* is **Michael Ondaatje**'s most important work, though he won the Governor General's Award and the Booker Prize for other books. His most recent volume of poetry is *Handwriting* and his most recent novel is *Anil's Ghost.**

P.K. Page is the author of over a dozen books of poetry, fiction, and non-fiction, and has been honoured with numerous awards, including the Governor General's Award for poetry. Recent publications include *The Hidden Room: Collected Poems* – two volumes (The Porcupine's Quill, 1997), *Compass Rose* – selected poems translated into Italian by Francesca Valente (Longo Editore, 1998), and *Alphabetical* (Hawthorne Society, 1998), winner of the bp nichol Chapbook Award. Her paintings have been exhibited internationally and she is represented in the permanent collections of The National Gallery of Canada, the Art Gallery of Ontario, and many other museums. Having travelled widely for much of her life, she now makes her home in Victoria.

Kenneth Radu lives near Montreal. A poet and novelist, his most recent publications include *Romanian Suite* (Brick Books) and Familiar Places (Véhicule).

Roberta Rees was born in New Westminster, B.C. She was raised in the village of Bellevue in the Crowsnest Pass, and now lives in Calgary where she has taught high school and university English courses and now teaches Creative Writing for Women. Her novel, *Beneath the Faceless Mountain*, was published in 1994. Roberta is currently working on a book of poetry and a novel.

John Reibetanz was born in New York City, and grew up in the eastern United States and Canada. He studied at the City University of New York and Princeton University, and has written essays on Elizabethan drama and on modern and contemporary poetry, as well as a book on King Lear and translations of modern German poetry. His poems have appeared in such magazines as *Poetry* (Chicago), *The Paris Review*, *Canadian Literature*, *The Malahat Review*, and *Quarry*, and twice in the anthology of winning entries to the National Poetry Competition. His previous collections, *Ashbourn* and *Morning Watch*, were published in the Signal Editions of Véhicule Press. He was a finalist for the 1995 National Magazine Awards, and has a new collection of poetry, *Mining for Sun*, due out with Brick Books in 2000. He lives in Toronto and teaches at Victoria College, where in 1989 he received the first Victoria University Teaching Award. His favourite non-literary pursuits are local history, contemporary art, and 1930's jazz.

William Robertson lives in Saskatoon. He teaches English in Prince Albert, Saskatchewan.

Robyn Sarah was born in New York City to Canadian parents, and has lived for most of her life in Montreal. Her poetry began appearing in Canadian literary magazines in the early 1970s, while she completed studies in philosophy at McGill University and music at the Conservatoire du Québec. She is the author of several previous poetry collections and two books of short stories.

Barbara Schott lives in Winnipeg, Manitoba, where she was born and raised. Her work as a fashion stylist frequently takes her to the Orient.

Her poetry has appeared in such literary journals as *TickleAce, Arc, Prairie Fire, Border Crossings* and *Contemporary Verse II*, and her chapbook *The Waterlily Pickers* was published by Turnstone Press. She was nominated for the 1997 John Hirsch Award For Most Promising Manitoba Writer, and won third place in the Bliss Carman Poetry Contest that same year. *Memoirs of an Almost Expedition* is her first full-length work.

Carolyn Smart is the author of four collections of poetry, and is currently working on a novel. She's taught Creative Writing at Queen's University since 1989 and works online with Writers in Electronic Residence. She lives in the country north of Kingston, Ontario with her husband and two boys.

Douglas Burnet Smith is the author of ten books of poetry. He teaches at Saint Francis Xavier University, and divides his time between Antigonish, Nova Scotia and Paris, France.

Francis Sparshott was born in England in 1926 and taught philosophy at the University of Toronto from 1950 until his retirement in 1991. He is married, has a daughter, and has published ten books of verse.

Colleen Thibaudeau was born in Toronto and has lived in Grey County, St. Thomas, Winnipeg and now London, Ontario. Her books include *My Granddaughters Are Combing Out Their Long Hair* and *The Martha Landscapes*. Her poems appear in many anthologies.

Lola Lemire Tostevin, translator of *Elimination Dance*, was born in Northern Ontario of French-speaking parents. She writes mainly in English and has published five collections of poetry, one novel and a collection of essays. Her translation of Anne Hébert's *Le Jour n'a d'égal qu la nuit* appeared in 1997.

A member of Renga, **David White** was born in London, Ontario in 1954. He was educated, off and on, at the University of Western Ontario and eventually completed a Ph.D. in 1994. He has been a factory worker, a janitor, a Summer Camp art instructor, a secretary, an assistant manager of a bookstore, a bar tender, and a college professor. He is currently teaching English at Fanshawe College. David still lives in London with Judy, Nick, and Shen. He has completed two novels which are resting comfortably in the bottom of a drawer somewhere in the house. And when time and his three-year-old daughter allow, he works away on novel number three.

Derk Wynand's *Closer to Home* (Brick Books, 1997) is his ninth collection of poetry. He has also published a collection of fiction and translations of books by the Austrian writers H.C. Artmann and Erich Wolfgang Skwara. He teaches at the University of Victoria.

Jan Zwicky's books include *Wittgenstein Elegies* (Brick Books, 1986), *The New Room* (Coach House, 1989), *Lyric Philosophy* (University of Toronto Press, 1992), and *Songs for Relinquishing the Earth* (Cashion, 1996; Brick Books, 1998), which won the 1999 Governor General's Award for Poetry. She has also published widely as an essayist on issues in music, poetry, and philosophy.

Brick Books in Print

0-919626-95-5   Crummey, Michael: *Hard Light* $12.95

0-919626-78-5   Curnoe, Greg: *Deeds/Abstracts* $16.95

1-894078-01-2   Davies, Lynn: *The Bridge That Carries the Road* $14.00

0-919626-14-9   Deane, Patrick et al.: *Renga* $6.00

0-919626-64-5   Dempster, Barry: *Letters from a Long Illness with the World: the D.H. Lawrence Poems* $11.95

0-919626-45-9   Donlan, John: *Domestic Economy* $9.95

0-919626-07-6   Dragišić, Peggy: *From the Medley* $3.00

0-88910-136-1   Dragland, Stan: *Peckertracks: a Chronicle* $12.95

0-88910-278-3   Dragland, Stan: *Journeys Through Bookland and Other Passages* $12.95

1-894078-10-1   Dragland, Stan, (ed.): *New Life in Dark Seas: Brick Books 25* $16.00

0-88910-400-x   Dragland, Stan: *The Bees of the Invisible: Essays in Contemporary English Canadian Writing* $15.95

0-919626-76-9   Dumont, Marilyn: *A Really Good Brown Girl* $12.95

0-919626-23-8   Dyck, E.F.: *Pisscat Songs* $7.50

0-919626-93-9   Friesen, Patrick: *A Broken Bowl* $12.95

0-919626-71-8   Geauvreau, Cherie: *Even the Fawn Has Wings* $11.95

0-919626-99-8   Goyette, Sue: *The True Name of Birds* $12.95

0-919626-74-2   Graham, Neile: *Spells for Clear Vision* $11.95

0-919626-20-3   Griggs, Terry: *Harrier* $3.50

0-919626-18-1   Gutteridge, Don: *God's Geography* $9.95

0-919626-51-3   Guttman, Naomi: *Reasons for Winter* $9.95

0-919626-42-4   Hall, Phil: *Amanuensis* $9.95

0-919626-87-4   Hall, Phil: *Hearthedral* $12.95

0-919626-60-2   Hall, Phil: *The Unsaid* $10.95

0-919626-26-2   Hall, Phil: *Why I Haven't Written* $8.50

0-919626-50-5   Hamilton, J.A.: *Body Rain* $9.95

0-919626-68-8   Hamilton, J.A.: *Steam-Cleaning Love* $11.95

0-919626-67-x   Harris, Maureen: *A Possible Landscape* $11.95

0-919626-77-7   Henderson, Brian: *Year Zero* $11.95

0-919626-84-x   Hoogland, Cornelia: *Marrying the Animals* $11.95

1-894078-02-0	Humphreys, Helen: *Anthem* $14.00
0-919626-29-7	Humphreys, Helen: *Gods and Other Mortals* $8.50
0-919626-47-5	Humphreys, Helen: *Nuns Looking Anxious, Listening to Radios* $9.95
0-919626-83-1	Humphreys, Helen: *The Perils of Geography* $11.95
0-919626-31-9	Kazuk, A.R.: *Microphones* $9.95
0-919626-97-1	Keefer, Janice Kulyk: *Marrying the Sea* $12.95
0-919626-48-3	Kenyon, Michael: *Rack of Lamb* $9.95
0-919626-92-0	Kerr, Don: *Autodidactic* $12.95
0-919626-34-3	King, Lyn: *The Pre-Geography of Snow* $8.50
0-919626-17-3	Kleinzahler, August, (ed.): *News and Weather* $9.95
0-919626-11-4	Kroetsch, Robert: *The Ledger* $8.95
0-919626-70-X	Lane, M. Travis: *Night Physics* $11.95
0-919626-91-2	Langille, Carole Glasser: *In Cannon Cave* $12.95
0-919626-90-4	Leckie, Ross: *The Authority of Roses* $12.95
0-919626-65-3	Lee, Dennis: *Riffs* $11.95
0-919626-81-5	Lee, Dennis: *Riffs (LargePrint Edition)* $14.00
0-919626-30-0	Lee, John B.: *Hired Hands* $9.95
0-919910-06-8	Lee, John B.: *Poems Only a Dog Could Love* $3.95
0-919626-41-6	Lee, John B.: *Rediscovered Sheep* $9.95
0-919626-19-X	Lee, John B.: *To Kill a White Dog* $5.95
0-919626-62-9	Lee, John B.: *Variations on Herb* $11.95
0-919626-39-4	Lilburn, Tim & Susan Shantz: *From the Great Above She Opened Her Ear to the Great Below* $16.95
0-919626-54-8	López-Pacheco, Jésus: *Poetic Asylum* $9.95
0-919626-16-5	Mackay, Brent: *The King of Bean* $5.50
0-919626-46-7	Maltman, Kim: *Technologies/Installations* $9.95
0-919626-73-4	Moritz, A.F.: *Mahoning* $11.95
1-894078-05-5	Moritz, A.F.: *Rest on the Flight into Egypt* $14.00
0-919626-57-2	Moritz, A.F.: *Song of Fear* $10.95
0-919626-82-3	Munro, Jane: *Grief Notes & Animal Dreams* $11.95
0-919626-55-6	Ondaatje, Michael: *Elimination Dance* $10.00
0-919626-79-3	Ondaatje, Michael: *Elimination Dance* (Large Print Edition) $10.00